STORIES F
AND S

STORIES FROM FOREST AND STEPPE

The Country Life of the Russian Countess

Edith Sollohub

First published 2014
by Impress Books Ltd
Innovation Centre, Rennes Drive, University of Exeter Campus, Exeter EX4 4RN

British Library Cataloguing in Publication Data

A catalogue record for this book is available from the British Library

ISBN 13: 978–1–907605–61–1 (pbk)
ISBN 13: 978–1–907605–62–8 (ebk)

Typeset in Garamond
by Swales and Willis Ltd, Exeter, Devon

Printed and bound in England
by imprintdigital.net

Countess Edith Sollohub came to England in 1939 to live with her son. She was accorded British citizenship in 1948, at the age of 62. This was her passport photograph.

CONTENTS

A NOTE FROM THE PUBLISHER

We are delighted to publish this second volume of Countess Edith Sollohub's memoirs, which we hope readers who enjoyed *The Russian Countess: Escaping Revolutionary Russia* will find equally fascinating. In many ways it offers a glimpse into the vanished world of turn-of-the-century rural Russia that has long since disappeared. It also places Edith's first memoir in the context of her earlier life, much of which was spent on the family's country estates. As you will discover, she reveals herself to be a strong, independent hunter, tracker, rider and countrywoman who eventually took on the full responsibility of running the estates. Many of these country skills and the fortitude needed to exercise them almost certainly contributed to the eventual success she had in escaping the Revolution and reuniting with her children in Estonia, a story so beautifully and grippingly told in *The Russian Countess*.

The stories you will find in this volume are mostly newly published. However, we have repeated some of the stories from Edith's previous book to place her memories of country life in context. Edith's memories focus on her time spent at Kamenka, Waldensee and Louisino (see map on p. x), the latter located near to the modern-day city of Kursk on the edge of the steppe. Each estate presented a different environment, culture and wildlife, reflected richly in Edith's writings.

Finally, we are indebted to Valerie Sollohub for bringing Edith's writings to us. As a publisher one always hopes for the opportunity to be able to publish rare and important literature and make it available to a wide and appreciative audience. Edith began writing her memoirs as soon as she escaped to Paris with her children in the 1920s and she, her son Nicolas and his wife Valerie spent many years editing her work and trying to find a publisher for it. The fact that we were able to do so is a privilege and we hope that their efforts have eventually been rewarded in the publication of these two volumes.

Richard Willis, Publisher, Impress Books
August 2014

Map showing position of the family estates

EARLY YEARS

1

CHILDHOOD VISITS TO WALDENSEE

I loved this house, Waldensee, which my father had bought so as to give us a country home. It was near Wolmar in Livonia, one of the Baltic provinces, and Father could make frequent visits there on his way to and from international conferences at The Hague which took up much of his time in the years leading up to The Hague Peace Conference of 1899. The conversation at table turned more and more to international events. The Spanish–American war broke out in 1898; we heard it discussed at table during lunch and the impression was stunning for sister Katya and me. We realised suddenly that history was not a thing of the past as we had thought, but that it was going on in our own time – though at a distance. I don't think I had any premonition of possible dangers, but my faith in history being just history and nothing more was gone. A feeling grew in me quite soon that things were changing, developing and that they might touch us too, however well we were sheltered in our parents' home. Reading some story which dealt with the great French Revolution I suddenly became terrified by the thought that things of that kind could also happen to us – and this thought never quite left me. Later, the revolutionary movement of 1904–5 in Russia brought back to my mind this fear of my childhood – an apprehension confirmed by the events of 1917. However, these dark thoughts did not spread any lasting shadows over me as a child and I think I enjoyed my childhood as fully as little girls of our circles could. And for me the summers in Waldensee were the best times of all.

The early mornings in our country home were so varied that I cannot select the best – they were all "best" in their own way. Our bedroom had closed wooden shutters but through the chinks I could see the sun, and then punctually at half past six my dog Kars managed to open the door (I suspect good old Niania helped him, as she could not resist the pleading eyes of a dog or a child). He was supposed to be a Siberian Laika, the dog that was used throughout Northern Siberia for tracking elk, lynx, ermine and squirrel. But poor Kars had a blemish in his pedigree: his ears did not stand up as they should, his tail curled up triumphantly and his paws were too small – to mention only a few of his faults. But I did not care, he was my devoted friend and the keenest dog I ever had. He would wake me by putting his front paws on my shoulders and poking his nose into my neck – I knew it meant "get up" and no call could have been more welcome. Dressing, washing, brushing my hair took little time, I fear, and Kars and I were soon out of the room leaving sister Katya still asleep. We ran (for we both always ran) to the stables to be on time for the grooming of the horses – blissful hours when I stood there under the heavy stone arches of the stables watching Ivan cleaning, brushing, trimming the horses, and the long friendly conversations we had then, all about horses and their tastes, nature and whims. As I loved horses I took it all in very keenly, and certainly learnt a lot during these hours, even though our conversation ran in infinitives as Ivan only spoke Latvian, which I did not know, and a sort of "short-hand" German. Sometimes the old father-in-law turned up and sat on an oak chest smoking his pipe and grunting some remarks which I could never understand, but he amused me because of his fear of horses: the moment one of them became restless, tickled by a brush or annoyed by a fly, the old man would quickly slip to the back of the chest, which served him as a protective bastion. By eight o'clock the horses were ready and happily munching their breakfast. Ivan had gone home for his coffee and I ran to the veranda where our breakfast was waiting. But on my way I stopped at the carnation beds to pick the prettiest one – a brilliant red or else a red and white striped one – to put on my father's plate for his button-hole.

After breakfast Father and I went round the "domain" as we called it: he wanted to have a look at the flower gardens, the hot-house, the stables and the fruit garden. I had so much to tell him then about the horses and the dogs, the fruit and the vegetables, and I wonder how he had the patience to listen to it all, or if he did not listen to let me chatter so. But as I think back now it must have been quite a help for him to learn about the wishes of Ivan and the thoughts of Ernest the gardener through me and not through them directly, as they both had great difficulty in expressing themselves in either Russian or German. As we passed through the kitchen garden and orchard I had to taste the new radishes, pulling them out of the ground and washing them in the dewy grass, or sample the gooseberries and currants. When the apple crop was ripe it meant tasting the apples, and with Father following my example we managed to eat quite a few fallen apples before we had done the rounds of the orchard. It was a lovely moment of the day with the long shadows of the trees falling on the grass-covered paths, with the dew still glistening on the longer blades, with the bees humming in the trees and the flower-beds of "flowers for cutting" looking a blaze of colour – the rows of asparagus plants framing them in light, feathery green.

It was also a blissful time because we had no regular lessons. The governess had no right to pin us down to books – and how I enjoyed this feeling of freedom. One of them had tried to limit my freedom at Waldensee by insisting on my telling her where I was going to be during the morning. But I soon found a way out of this trouble by reciting to her the names of all the places I possibly could be – with the result that she never could know where I actually was, and she soon gave up asking me.

But there were also very different mornings in the country when I reached fourteen and was allowed to go alone to our small woods across the fields. They too ended at eight o'clock when Father wanted me to be there for breakfast with him. But they started at dawn, and Kars was my companion, along with the Montecristo, my brother's little rifle. Those were perfect mornings with the sun just rising, with the mists lingering over the low, wet meadows, with the stubble fields grey with cobwebs. The run across the fields was short, the path straight and Kars kept to "heel" as long as there was no temptation. The moment we approached the little forest which stretched in a narrow band along the river, Kars was off like a dart and I saw no sign of him until I heard him barking up a tree after a squirrel. The excitement began then: Kars jumped up at the trunk of a tree, panting and following with his sharp eyes any movement in the branches. The squirrel, tired or frightened by the barking, jumped from tree to tree and Kars, following it, barked in a high distressed voice all along the course while I tried to shoot the squirrel, firing bullet after bullet until I finally brought it down. Then, we both dashed for it. If Kars was first I was really in a plight for he would not let me touch the prey, but I insisted on having it in order to cut off the tail, for which I would get a premium of 20 kopeks, the usual reward given to the gamekeepers. How many times Kars bit me – involuntarily, I am sure – as we struggled for possession of the poor dead squirrel! How many times I came home dangling the squirrel tails tied with dry blades of grass and hiding the handkerchief tied round a bleeding hand or arm, in fear of the governess making a scene over it and stressing the importance of disinfection, the danger of dogs' bites, and so on. But never mind – Kars and I had had our sport and we came home hot and tired, creeping round the back of the stables to my room for a quick tidy-up before breakfast. Unforgettable mornings which gave me so much joy, which taught me to shoot accurately, to share the keen sporting spirit of my dogs, and to rely upon myself.

On warm summer days it was not easy to make up one's mind about the next morning: would it be the forest and shooting or would it be the river and fishing? Of course my fishing was the most primitive affair: I knew few fish, I knew very little about their tastes and habits and just as little about the baits and the hooks. But I loved fishing in the primitive way that I used to do it, either with Father fishing before sunset from the little bridge or my fishing alone on the lake which fascinated me. At sunrise again, Kars and I would leave the house cautiously; I took the heavy oars, my fishing tackle and a bucket for bailing the water out of the boat and off we went to the forest, then through it to the river where the boat was chained. On the bank, in the soft murky earth there were enough worms to fill my little box in a few minutes; a large stone which served as an anchor was hidden in the nearby bushes, and we could set out undisturbed, rowing downstream in the shade of the huge dark spruce growing on our bank of the river.

After a mile and a half the river widened, becoming a sort of lake with wide belts of rushes reaching far into the distance. This is where I dropped anchor and settled down to fish, with Kars curled up for a snooze in the bottom of the boat if it was dry enough or on the wider seat in the bows. And I fished, fished patiently for hours and very rarely caught anything. But it was so beautiful on the glassy surface of the lake, it was so fascinating watching the wild duck families starting their day's hunt for food among the reeds, it was so quiet and so far from anybody that I enjoyed every minute and rowed home reluctantly, annoyed to have to return to the hustle and bustle of everyday life. Only Kars was disappointed on those mornings for he saw that I carried no gun, and crossing through the forest he looked longingly at the trees hoping to spy a squirrel.

There were some special dates during the summer months in Waldensee that provided us children with a lot of excitement, fun and interest. In fact, these dates had more meaning for the grown-ups as they were those of traditional festivities in the various estates of the neighbourhood and we children generally participated only in those which took place in our own house. But even when our parents and their friends staying at our house were going to one of these big parties (generally dinners at 7.30, sometimes tea at 4.30 followed by the dinner party) we had a lot of fun. I spent hours before the departure watching the coachman Ivan polishing, dusting, inspecting all the harnesses and carriages, giving a last brushing to the seats, a last stroke of a brush with some mysterious tar-smelling stuff on some parts of the wheels. It was fascinating to watch him, and when Lisa, his wife, joined him and brushed his livery and the funny coachman's cap and stretched on her hands the gloves she had just washed for him – then I knew that it was time to watch for the most interesting part of the show, the harnessing of the four-in-hand. I was terribly proud of this four-in-hand and had no eyes any more for the usual caleche which followed the big landau and which had only two horses – one of them even being the farmer's horse. On these days Ivan did not allow us to climb into the carriage and drive round to the front door – our shoes would soil the carpet. So I ran behind the carriage and enjoyed this run just as much as I did the usual ride. It was grand to see the four horses pull on, the gardener's boy holding the front pair who never could start without prancing about. Ivan had his most serious face; his beard lay well brushed like a red fan on his chest, his long whip, the new one, stood up like a mast in front of him and all the metal parts of the harness were so glittering, so bright that the sun played on them and they sent sparks on the steps of the terrace.

Father stood ready – always the first and always on time – with his light summer suit and brown soft hat and my carnation in his buttonhole. Mother came out looking so elegant and pretty in her light foulard dress, with her white shoes and large white hat with masses of ostrich feathers on it. I admired her and thought that fortunately there were many years still to pass before I would have to get into such clothes and hats and gloves. I patted my scruffy sailor shirt and felt the supply of apples in its deep recesses and was thoroughly happy.

My mother's birthday on the 27th July was the occasion for us to return hospitality to our Baltic friends. Long skirts, large-brimmed hats with scores of hat pins fixing them to buns, curls and rolls of hair, a little powder and no rouge – this is what I see when I think of my mother's birthday party at Waldensee.

Fortunately the long skirts did not concern me at the time, nor did the hats, and my mane of thick brown hair was held together by a ribbon – white for the festivity. Brilliant sunshine in the early morning when, after my daily visit to the stables where Ivan was grooming the horses, I had to be in good time for breakfast. Mother in her white silk dressing gown sat in the chair highly decorated with branches of lime trees and many flowers. She looked like some Eastern deity amongst these wild shades of green and bright colours. The table was covered with flowers and there was the big birthday cake in the shape of a "Bretzel" surrounded by red and white carnations. How promising the almonds half baked into its surface looked now, and how impatiently I waited for the opportune moment to slip my knife into the chink of the fattest almond, to snap off the top half of it, if my governess did not catch me in this manoeuvre. But fortunately she was too long admiring Mother's presents – all put around Mother's place – the jewels from Father, some paintings from sister Katya, some jig-saw work of my production, books, vases from other members of the household. The almonds off the cake were awfully good, my brother competed with me, and Father gave us a warning glance – better stop for the time being. We heard murmuring and shuffling of feet on the gravel outside and then the high-pitched voices of the women on the farm singing song after song, with words unknown to us, but all in praise of Mother. Their white kerchiefs gleamed in the sunshine, they were half hidden by the herbaceous border in full bloom, their voices were so shrill but never a wrong note even in the audacious chords and variations to which two or three men's voices gave a droning background. Mother thanked them from the steps of the terrace, and patted the heads of the blue-eyed fair-haired children clinging to the embroidered aprons of the younger women. The shrivelled yellow-faced babka (old woman), Ivan's mother, laughed and cracked a joke apparently; we missed it, but all laughed heartily.

It was a lovely day; we were enjoying everything. Brother Kolya was finishing the most complicated arrangements for the evening's illuminations: fireworks and paper lanterns were fixed in intricate designs all along wires drawn across the lawn between the rows of lime trees and all along the drive. Katya and I helped him eagerly and ran up and down stairs with loads of lanterns, candles, sticks and hooks. Kolya wanted more sticks, his fireworks were to be grander than ever – and I ran off to the little wood to cut young elders in the thicket. Kars was at my heel but he did not bark joyously for he saw that I had no gun – not much fun, he thought. And how lovely the wood was, teeming with life – insects, flies and birds filling it with their sounds. Kars was off – he barked furiously and jumped up along the trunk of a pine tree. I tried to see where the squirrel went – for it was always a squirrel when Kars behaved like that – the elder sticks could wait; and we followed, Kars and I, the squirrel in its flight from tree to tree. I craned my neck to see it in the top branches of a transparent luminous birch; I screwed up my face and looked through my fists when it disappeared in a dark spruce. Kars was exhausted, panting like an engine, drops fell from his flapping pink tongue and his golden-brown eyes looked at me pathetically: "Why don't you get it?" they seemed to ask.

We must go – get the sticks – I patted Kars, talked to him and showed my empty hands. "No gun – nothing . . ." and we went back on the soft carpet of thick dark green moss, back into the thicket where my sticks lay on a bed of twigs and leaves that I had already stripped off. How strong the smell of freshly cut wood was in the morning, how it mixed with the heavy scent coming from the peat-bog close by.

The weather was too lovely. We could not miss our swim in the river and, leaving all further preparations for the afternoon, we went off to the river. The men were there already – we had to wait for them to come up the path through the wood where Mother had had a bench put, "belle vue" as we called it. It really was a pretty view, over the tops of trees from a sand cliff, along the shaded brook and towards soft slopes of fields with a few farm buildings hidden among apple trees. We thoroughly enjoyed the brisk swim in a cold stream. From the steps of the bathing hut our governess corrected our swimming and counted the seconds we took to swim to the old spruce which had slid down the sand cliff the previous spring and now hung low over the surface of the water. The brook was dark green there and shoals of little fish swam in and out of the hollows under the tree's arched roots. The sun made bright round spots and the red sand of the cliff was reflected in ever-moving ripples at the bend of the brook. There were crawfish there, but as I could not dive I couldn't lift the stones under which they hid.

Luncheon that day was particularly good – fortunately the special delicacies, ordered from Petersburg, arrived in time; the chef had produced marvellous "pirog" cake, and the well-cooled hock was much appreciated by us all, with the exception of sister Mary. She sat next to Mother, her plate surrounded by pet toys – all animals – who came in turn to attend at meals; not more than three at a time was the law put down by Mother.

By three o'clock all arrangements for the illuminations and fireworks were ready and we looked anxiously at the sky where a few long puffy clouds had appeared. Our governess – after her nap – came out to see that we got ready in good time, for although the neighbours were invited to dinner some of them had already arrived. These were generally the very distant neighbours who were a good two or three hours' distance from us and whose horses would need a long rest before they started on the homeward trip. The nearest neighbours were some two miles off and they too frequently came early, to have a game of tennis or because the old gentleman was particularly anxious to chat with Father and Mother and could not do so to his heart's content when all the other guests were assembled.

Niania was waiting in our bedroom to do our hair. She brushed it down energetically, especially mine which always seemed terribly tangled and full of moss, twigs and leaves. The white frocks lay on the beds, the coloured belts hung on the back of the chair, the shoes were so distressingly white – useless for the dewy evening grass when the fireworks started. Kars pricked up his ears as he lay near my bed, and I heard the distant rumbling of wheels over the wooden bridge down the drive. Katya and I hurriedly buckled the belts, pinned the brooches and made a little bet between ourselves as to who the first guests would be. From our narrow window on the west side we could see the avenue down to the first hill. There was movement there: a carriage – whose horses? Knieriem? No, Kokenhof! No, Rantzen! . . . we called out in turn trying to guess the owners by the colour of the horses. Well, it was Rantzen: the four heavy black horses, the spacious landau and the coachman we disliked as he always looked grumpy and hit his horses.

On the terrace Father and Mother greeted the guests. Father was so smart in his light grey suit with the light tie and the pearl pin in it. In his buttonhole he wore the deep red carnation I gave him that morning. Mother was lovely as usual in her blue pastel foulard dress with a long gold and sapphire chain round her neck. Of course Kolya was not ready – I saw him peeping over the edge of the window upstairs, pulling his tie straight and still in shirt sleeves. Even on Mother's birthday he couldn't be ready on time.

As a rule the first guests were older people who were quickly left to the care of the parents. Little by little all of the expected visitors turned up and often enough they brought with them their friends who might be staying with them at the moment, so that one never quite knew how many people would actually be seated at table. When there were young people we took them round the garden, the stables, for a sail on the pond in a very shaky little boat, and even for a quick walk in my beloved little forest.

Well, the dinner went along its usual lines: Mother's health was drunk with champagne after the first speech made by one of her two neighbours, the two who always sat on her right and on her left and who always competed with each other as to who was to snatch the right moment for that speech. Mother looked very pretty, the flowers on both tables were lovely, many more flowers filled the vases as each guest had brought a huge bunch; the speeches flowed easily and we, the young ones, went round the table touching our glasses of champagne with the older people or stood up singing "Hoch soll sie leben". As soon as it got dark Kolya started the fireworks while we lit the paper lanterns all round the house and in the garden. The men sat on the terrace sipping their drinks and smoking; the women – well I don't know where they were; and the young people ran round the garden seeing to the lanterns which caught fire with a gust of wind, or just walked and chatted. Then came the horrid moment when Father called me and told me to "play something". I dutifully took out my violin, Mother sat down at the piano, the guests crowded into the sitting room, the study and the small salon. Only a few of the older men were independent enough to stay where they were over their drink. And then I started; how I hated it, and how I must laugh at it all now, half a century later. But then it was the thing to do, I could not protest, but I felt that Mother quite shared my feelings. However, Father was pleased and so proud of my playing that the performance had to be gone through – finishing with Grieg's "An den Frühling", which was a piece I really loved and which made me forget the unpleasantness of the moment.

As well as being beautiful, my mother was also very talented, with an interest in music, literature and painting. I could catch glimpses of Mother's world through the person of Akavavna, my mother's Russian governess. Her name was in fact Alexandra Nikolayevna Velsovskaya, but this was too long for us children and we contracted it into "Akavavna". She was a dumpy, lively little woman with black eyes, no figure and a strong limp. I loved her for her endless stories and fairytales which she could tell or read in the same even, clear voice without ever getting tired. She often read aloud to my mother while Mother was painting; she read fast and equally well in Russian and French, and they generally stopped at the end to discuss the chapters just read. Her tone was clear and keen and I am sure that her judgements must have been worth noting: there was nothing futile, superficial or haphazard in her tone. Both Father and Mother had the greatest respect for her and often discussed the latest trend of literature with her. I know that it is from these discussions that I got my first ideas about Turgenev, Tolstoy and the later modern writers.

The servants at Waldensee, were they loyal Russian subjects even though Russian was a language they scarcely spoke? Their world was so close to ours, but for us it was a world that remained largely unexplored. I feel very fortunate that in thinking of all these people there is not the faintest taint of bitterness in my recollections and certainly a great deal of gratitude towards many among them. The regret arises that I may not always have appreciated the kindness, devotion and patience of many old servants, probably because it was all taken for granted. But looking back now after many years and from entirely different surroundings, I see more clearly the human element in our relations with our servants, both in the Baltics and in Russia, and realise that we, too, were taken for granted in a way and the servants would not have had us different from what we were. Of course, there were a few among our servants who changed their attitude towards us – who withdrew from our horizon and were swallowed up in the rising tide of "conscious citizens" as they thought they had become, thanks to the revolution. But these were only few, and came from among those who had not been personally well known to us – they were not old servants. And, after all, would one blame them? They had to face their families, their surroundings with the new ideas; and with curses being showered upon us, they were looked at askance for having been in our service, for having protected our property against the new upcoming class. Some vanished discreetly, afraid of coming across us but never seeming to have been active against us. A few became openly hostile.

But all these things were far in the future and unimaginable in those sheltered childhood years. Year after year we returned to our dear Waldensee. By the time I was seventeen, I was the proud possessor of a delightful 20-calibre shotgun – the Christmas present from Mother and Father when they finally and reluctantly gave in to my request. Of course there was no shooting for me in winter while we were still in Petersburg. I waited more impatiently than ever for the spring, to go to the country, to try my new gun. And finally we were there and finally, too, the shooting season opened. After June 29th the ducks on the lake had no peace – I was down hiding in rushes whenever I could escape Kars' watchful eye. He was excellent with squirrels but he still had no idea about water fowl and rushed right down into the water with much splashing and noise whenever he spied duck anywhere.

Then came the real shooting season – my first with a proper gun – after September 1st, when I was invited to the real shoots together with my brother, and when he and I wandered off every morning at 6 a.m. for a private shoot with our large, inefficient and disobedient golden pointer, Nimrod. We trudged through forests and woods, moors and swamps, rarely bringing home anything but a stray moor-hen or a hare at best, but the satisfaction was great and I learnt a lot, training my eye to follow the birds I had not paid much attention to before – my game having been squirrels until then.

One day we were invited to a regular shooting party, starting early in the morning. By 6 a.m. my brother and I were on the road. I was driving my favourite horse, Miru, in the small, light four-wheeler and we arrived on time to join the rest of the party. To our annoyance we could only stay for the morning, since we were required to return home soon after midday. Still, we enjoyed the shooting; the hares were scarce as they usually were on this estate, but I was alone on the stand and this meant a lot of exciting moments anyhow. By noon we were ready to go home and left with our guns well packed in their cases. I was driving again, as Kolya highly disliked horses and anything connected with them. The distance was not great – some five

14

miles – along the high road first and then along a small forest road for a short cut.

We were rolling briskly along the last bit of the high road, which dipped here into a small valley through which ran a brook with wooded banks – hazelnut bushes in fact – when I noticed three men with double-barrelled guns crossing the road from the field above and disappearing into the brushwood. They were not known to me, and this struck me as strange for the shooting rights were very strictly upheld in these parts of the country and I knew the few people who had the right to go shooting here. I told Kolya to look at them carefully so that we could report these men to the gamekeeper of the place; and at that very moment three shots resounded one after the other in quick succession. Our brown mare bolted forward as the shots came from close by, from the bushes to the left. I held the reins tighter to straighten her but let her go as fast as she could. My brother looked round rather puzzled: "Do you think that was meant for us?" he asked slowly. "I don't see for whom else, after all," was my reply, "there's not much game in these bushes right beside the road." We drove up the hill, turned to the right and from the ridge there I could see the three men standing at the edge of the brushwood, their guns on their backs.

Our coachman Ivan, when told about the occurrence, shook his head and said, "Times are getting bad, you must not drive alone, Miss Edy, as you generally do – one never knows." I did not like the idea of having my beloved drives or rides curtailed.

The same evening a friend of ours drove his carriage drawn by two horses along the same high road some five or six miles further up. As the road led through a dense pine forest, five shots fell, all from shotguns, and riddled the hood of the carriage, stuck in the coachman's thick coat and grazed the man's hand. We concluded that this was the work of the same three men who had first tried their luck on us.

All too soon we were near the end of this, my first shooting season as a fully-fledged "gun". One day, which had been very unsatisfactory with little game and few shots as the dogs seemed to be bent on chasing the hares round and round outside the area where the guns were posted, I found myself sharing a stand with our neighbour Konrad Knieriem. It was a quiet and colourful October day, the forests looked friendly and still smelled of mushrooms (or, rather, toadstools as the season of edible mushrooms was over). Kolya and I had been invited to go shooting with Konrad and I was enjoying every minute of it – the only sad note being the thought that in two days' time we were to leave Waldensee and go to Petersburg for the winter as usual. I tried not to think of it and to enjoy these last moments as one can enjoy things so intensely when one is eighteen.

Konrad, our host, was sharing the stand with me as the line had to be shortened in this last beat – and there was not much game to be expected by then. I quite liked Konrad after all: he was six years my senior, the age of my brother. He liked shooting and riding and was probably very kind. He was now in charge of running his father's estate and was keen on improving it. His looks . . . well he certainly was not attractive with his rather stuffed figure, arms sewn on to a body that looked as though it had just come from the upholsterer. Black hair and a small dark moustache, above which hung such a long, sad nose! He had a fascinating way of twiddling his moustache right and left when he felt self-conscious – and this happened very often. He was shy and quiet, he had never anything much to say and fully realised that this was a drawback when at a party. However, when he and I were together he always managed to chat quite happily, telling me all about his horses and dogs, his farm plans and his shooting. There were also other topics of conversation with him and my father always teased me for managing to draw something out of Konrad the silent.

There we were, waiting for a stray hare to slip away from the hounds barking somewhere in the distance. And we chatted in subdued tones keeping a sharp eye on the glade in front of us. But conversation did not flow easily today. Poor Konrad had even less to say than usual and I tried to find the dog–gun–horse topic which would wake him up. Giving up my attempts as of no avail, I mentioned again, probably for the tenth time, how sad I was to go away to Petersburg. This time Konrad suddenly became quite voluble trying to make me a glowing picture of the lovely life I should have now, just grown up and in the capital (where

he himself had never been). I was not so sure that I liked the idea
of grand balls and big parties, having always feared the moment
when that life would have to be faced. And I went on repeating
how much I preferred my country home and country life which
seemed so much simpler and clearer to me.

"You really prefer the country?" said Konrad after a moment's
silence, his whiskers twiddling frantically under his long nose.
"Yes, I do, even though there is so much that I love also in town
– music for instance." The whiskers stopped twiddling; Konrad
was obviously thinking and then said, "You know, you need
not leave the country – you could stay . . ." I laughed. "Alone?
I don't think it would do, even though I would not mind it."
Konrad's whiskers became frantically agitated. "No – not alone
– the decision is with you . . . you could stay!" I looked away a
bit worried. This sounded strange, too incoherent for Konrad's
normal way of expressing himself, and the little blue eyes peered
intensely at me.

Poor Konrad, he did not know what to say next. We were
silent; from the corner of my eye I could see the agitation of his
whiskers – too funny and pathetic – and what did he mean, really?
I felt too shy to ask him to explain.

The dogs came to our rescue. The favourite, Turco, managed
to chase a hare towards us. "Shoot!" I called. "There on the right!"
Konrad obediently levelled his gun, shot – and missed. "How
stupid – I think it was an easy shot?" said Konrad, disconcerted.
"I don't know, perhaps you could not see it well," I put in, still in
a daze after our strange conversation. "Of course, I should have
let you shoot, you must have more practice, you must stay here!
Won't you? . . ." and the whiskers started anew and the little blue
eyes looked kind. "Yes, I do need practice – I'll try . . ." and I saw
to my relief the gamekeeper and my brother coming up the ride.

Was it an offer of marriage? Looking back I think I see now
that that was what he meant – and I do not regret that the question
remained unanswered.

2

MARRIAGE AND MOVING
TO KAMENKA

By the summer of 1906 I was engaged to be married to Count
Alexander Sollohub, my friend Sasha with whom I spent happy
times on the skating rink and tennis court. My parents were to let
us have an apartment in town, and for our country house there
was Kamenka, a property that Sasha had bought some 80 versts
(50 miles) to the south of Petersburg.

Sasha's childhood had been very different from my own. He
was born on his family's estate, Louisino, near Kursk, on May
1st, 1884. When he was four years old his father fell ill, was taken
to Moscow and died there. His mother took him to Moscow
with her at that time, but afterwards they returned to Louisino
where his mother stayed all year round, working hard and
managing the estate.

When Sasha was about twelve years old, he was taken to
Voronezh to school, and he lived there every winter with
his mother until he was seventeen. At seventeen he came to
Petersburg, passed his exams and entered the 4th Class of the
Lyceum – the last "silver collar" class. He worked well and loved
his time at the Lyceum, living partly at home and partly at school
– as the boys were expected to live there. He was "General ot
Fronta" when he came into the 1st Class (the highest one), with a
golden collar and sword. His duty was to see to the discipline, to
take parades of all boys when any ceremony took place, to review
them all every day as they filed into the dining hall for meals, and
to see – as far as possible – that all boys behaved properly when

out of the school and kept strictly to regulations in clothes and manners. When meeting in the street, the boys gave the military salute; they were never allowed to wear civilian clothes, could not go to restaurants (at any rate, not into the large public rooms), had to wear white gloves, button up all the buttons on their uniform coats, and were only allowed to wear their small winter caps if the thermometer went below 15°C. Sasha loved all these traditions and took them all very seriously.

In 1903, or about that time, Sasha bought Kamenka from a big industrialist named Franz Franzevitch Utemann. As his mother could not manage both places, and as she was very attached to Louisino where she had worked all these years, an uncle was entrusted with the superintendence of Kamenka. A permanent manager was placed there, with the uncle being supposed only to give general directions. The uncle held this post for three years and was well paid for it, but managed to get to Kamenka only twice – once to shoot elk, and another time for the capercailzie shooting in spring. He did not take the work seriously and allowed such misusage that the whole place was on the verge of ruin when Sasha took it over himself in 1906.

In the spring of that year Sasha finished at the Lyceum with the 2nd Gold Medal. And in June we became engaged and Sasha decided that he would now take over Kamenka, leaving Louisino to his mother. He would also enter state service – as the boys from the Lyceum were expected to do – and join the Imperial Chancellery, where they had plenty of leisure and were not obliged to be present. His service there never lasted more than a few weeks each year, and dwindled down to casual visits from time to time. Eventually Sasha decided not to go on with the work there, for Kamenka needed all his attention.

Sasha's mother insisted on my going to see my future home, and Sasha was keen on my coming there in October for a two-day shoot. So we were packed off, sister Katya and I, and joined my future mother-in-law at the Nikolayevsky station. The old lady was certainly very impressive, with her stern expression on a decidedly ugly face – with large features and a mass of grey hair. She walked slowly, held herself very straight and had very little to say at any time.

We took the train to Tosno, and after that there was a three-hour drive from the station – sitting in silence and feeling weighed down by the grey, damp autumnal weather. The forests bordering the road never seemed to end and when we at last reached open fields I had a sense of relief: more space, more free breathing, I thought. And there stood Kamenka: no impressive castle (I had not expected it to be), but a cosy looking wooden two-storied shooting lodge sheltered from the north by huge fir trees and overlooking a sort of lawn, in the centre of which stood an enormous lime tree. Very soon this would be my home. I wondered . . . and preferred not to think in advance. In a haze of impressions I walked round the place, visited the stables, the manège which impressed me a lot, the huge cow-house looking like a Chinese pagoda, the abandoned uncared-for garden which seemed to have great possibilities, and in the same haze I duly talked at dinner and spent the evening in the red salon, until finally it was bedtime.

What a relief to go to sleep and to forget the problems which I felt now beginning to surge up around me. How should I behave, now that I was engaged? Was this the right thing to say? Was that the right thing to do? Should I smile all the time? Should I ask endless questions on running a house, on caring for cows and pigs? Was I still myself, or did I have to creep head and all into the mould prepared for me, duly bearing the label "Girl happy – getting married next month"? This label crushed me, crippled me, for how would I be able to live up to the expectations of all the people surrounding me? Enough to make anyone downcast, when I think of it now. Still – I knew I had to bravely face my new life and the duties looming on the horizon, and try to ignore those worrying thoughts that kept reappearing at odd moments when I was alone.

There I was, a complete stranger and complete novice in everything concerned with running a house, facing my future mother-in-law and the household of servants at Kamenka. Everyone looked at me inquiringly as if sizing me up and drawing their own conclusions. Fortunately at the time I was not in the least conscious of evil-minded and suspicious natures or of gossip-loving tongues, and only thought of the tasks facing me and of the proper way of facing them. Obviously a sense of duty had been well drilled into us as children. Perhaps the austere looks of my future mother-in-law accentuated all these apprehensions and robbed me of the modest ration of self-assurance that I may have had. Anyhow, the hours in the house dragged slowly on, the conversation seemed to be stretched out over topics of dogs and horses, but even there I felt a novice and all I said seemed limp and pretty helpless.

The early morning departure for a day's shoot with beaters was a huge relief. The old lady presided over the breakfast and saw us off: Sasha, the estate manager Baron Fersen and myself – we were only three guns. Sister Katya, who did not care for shooting, remained at home and I knew she would find plenty of things to do or to interest her in and out of the house.

The day's shoot was thrilling and exciting. The enormous stretches of forests were new to me; the vast moors over thousands of acres impressed me; and the variety of game was fascinating. Of course I shot badly: waiting for a hare I was suddenly called upon to shoot at a hazel hen and hesitated which barrel to use in accordance with the number of the cartridge in them; or then a neat swish of wings would resound immediately after the first call of the beaters and I was too late to aim at the lovely huge capercailzie passing over my head. On taking our places at another stand Sasha would tell me: "Mind, keep a good look out for there might be elk in this drive, but don't shoot them as you may make a mistake and shoot at an elk cow. Besides, your 20-calibre gun with shot is not really suitable for big game," and I would be left there trembling with terror and wondering what to do if an elk really came out near me! To shoot a cow would have been a never-forgotten shame, and to miss any game would mean bringing shame on Sasha that he had chosen such a clumsy girl for his wife. But to let it pass – as if unnoticed – would be just as bad with all these beaters and gamekeepers looking on. I must admit that I was glad when the last beat was over . . . and my little achievements did not look bad. It had been a very tiring day, but I did not dare admit it either to Katya or to myself.

The next day was perhaps less worrying but no less tiring as it rained steadily and the wet clothes weighed such a lot towards evening. By that time Katya had had a good look at the library and after dinner she eagerly pointed out to me many interesting publications which in later years became great friends of mine.

Summing up these two days in my mind I felt grateful that things had gone smoothly, that I had not shot an elk cow nor missed too good a shot at capercailzies; also, I had not shown signs of my tiredness and my future mother-in-law had been as gracious – and, at the same time, as distant – as she could be. But I had the feeling that Katya did not have great illusions about the "pleasant character" of the old lady. Baron Constantin Fersen and his wife had been quite cheerful and supplied a "third element" in an atmosphere which without them might have been a little strained. They had been married only two years. The Baron was a gentle, hesitant but friendly man, and his wife was a girl whom I had met before her marriage at the house of our nearest neighbours at Waldensee. Although we had not really been friends we had many topics of conversation in common, and this had helped during the dinners and evenings at Kamenka.

Early on the third day we duly left, Katya and I in the first carriage and Sasha with his mother in the second. Three good hours of steady trot brought us to Tosno station, and after an hour and twenty minutes in the train we were in Petersburg. Our old coachman was waiting for us at the station – and I felt really relieved and happy to get home.

In my heart I felt somehow guilty and ungrateful. Surely I should have had an effervescent feeling of happiness? I should have been elated at having seen my future home. And yet I just could not rouse these feelings in my heart. The most pleasant impressions for me had been the shooting trips into the endless silent forests and – as far as home was concerned – the large stables, the riding school, the smell of horses and harness. The people had been pleasant to me but at the same time all so distant and so scrutinising – at least so it had seemed on this first visit.

We were married on Sunday, November 12th, 1906, at the Lyceum Church and travelled at once to Kamenka for our honeymoon. Rather the wrong setting for a honeymoon, with the absence of sun, with the cold and damp, and the grey short hours of daylight. But we had both been abroad with our families that summer, and at Kamenka we could make the most of enjoying the shooting season.

We were married on Sunday, and today it was Tuesday. It was all very new to me – so unfamiliar in its quietness, in the absence of music and of the various interests which had, until now, filled my days in Petersburg. To my relief, the household seemed to run by itself. The house was warm and spacious, there were plenty of interesting books, and we both sat reading – reading and waiting. We were waiting, I was told, for the gamekeepers to come to report at about noon. What they were to report about I did not exactly know, and I dared not ask. So we just waited and read – not very attentively on my part. I was tired of sitting, and had been waiting ever since breakfast. But I had not had the courage to go out for a stroll, as Sasha had decided: "We must stay here and wait." Fortunately, there was a delightful dog, the white Samoyed, Belka, who had immediately adopted me, and who now wagged her tail when I smiled at her as she lay curled on the brightly coloured oriental carpet. What a beauty she was, with her large, brown, expressive eyes. And the eyes said now: "Come out for a walk, won't you?" And the tail wagged quicker and the black nose seemed to move, sniffing for fresh air.

"I think Belka would like to go out for a stroll, don't you? Might we not take her out a little?" Sasha looked up from his book. "By all means, take her out in the garden. You'll find your way?" He smiled. "I'll stay here and wait."

Yes, I had forgotten this "wait". But Belka had understood about the walk and was up and alert. I must go; she was too delightfully confident, and I could not let her down. A few minutes later we were out in the garden and at the foot of the hillock in the meadow where no one could see us, and I ran with Belka as I always used to with my own Kars in Waldensee. I came back along the foot of the hillock, and then walked demurely up to the top with Belka still jumping round me asking for more fir cones and sticks to be thrown for her. Dear Belka! How many times she cheered me.

In the warm and cosy red drawing room Sasha was still reading, with piles of books at his side. He looked up as I came in, and smiled. "You liked your walk? None of the men has come yet, and it's nearly noon. We'll have to wait." And he was back in his book. I also picked up a book, and Belka licked herself clean with discreet noises.

A tap at the door. "Come in!" said Sasha, putting aside his book and looking eagerly at the door. Our estate manager Baron Fersen sidled in, pushing his pince-nez into place.

"Sidor has just come, and he reports that some five or six elk – two of them males, he thinks – are in the Kudrovskaya Dacha, district no. 27, I think . . ." said the Baron in hesitating tones.

"Good. Thank you, Baron. Perhaps you would kindly send Sidor here – I want to give him his orders. You'll come with us, won't you?"

"With the greatest pleasure. Thank you. You see, when I last saw elk, three weeks ago, I think . . . or was it a month . . ."

"Did you? Oh, I see. But would you kindly send Sidor? I must give him orders at once, as it is already late." Sasha seemed quite used to dealing with the Baron's slow and never-ending sentences.

"Of course, of course, no time to be lost – with elk in particular. Yes, we'll be ready . . ." and, sidling somewhat more quickly, he disappeared through the doorway.

Sasha turned to me apologetically. "You'll see, he is a good fellow, but not very quick. I sometimes wonder how he will run the place here."

A knock at the door and Sidor, the head gamekeeper at Kamenka, came in with his straggly yellow hair brushed well back behind his ears, his moustache drooping. His report was apparently quite satisfactory, although I couldn't quite make it all out. Anyhow, no more waiting. Luncheon was to be served immediately, and we were to start at one o'clock.

Everything worked to perfection. The luncheon was not underdone, my clothes were right and ready, the boots well oiled. Sidor had laid out the cartridge belts in the hall and seen to the guns, and at one o'clock exactly we got into a light sledge, Sasha driving. There was really too little snow for a sledge, but the deep, hard-frozen ruts would have been too much for the wheels and springs of a light dogcart. So we were jerked and shaken and thrown right and left, with the sledge creaking and groaning, and the horse sliding and stumbling, and Sasha using language which sounded pretty bad to me.

The beaters and the gamekeepers were waiting at the spot where the sledges were to be left. All eyes were turned on me, and all mouths gaped open wide, for here was the new mistress, who went shooting with her husband – a thing almost unheard of – and who even used a gun. This was something really new.

In the meantime, instructions were given in muffled voices; the Baron fussed about with the reels of red flags; Sasha adjusted his thick-rimmed shooting glasses – and we set off in single file along the narrow ride. There were to be two stands only, for, being totally inexperienced with elk, I was to remain with Sasha. The Baron drew the first number, and I noticed that Sidor smiled under his moustache. I guessed that the second stand must be the better one, and the Baron did not seem to be a great favourite with the people.

We had not waited very long before the beaters started. Their shouts seemed to advance like a wall, slowly, steadily, straight towards us. I stood a stride or two behind Sasha, not daring to move and feeling certain that I could never hear the elk amidst all the noise made by the beaters.

All of a sudden I saw Sasha stretch out his neck and peer intently into the undergrowth in front of us. A distressing sort of undergrowth, looking light and sparse, but so muzzy and confusing in the variety of grey and green patches that I could not distinguish anything. Suddenly, Sasha levelled his gun and shot. At last I saw large, dark shapes moving swiftly between the young aspen and willow bushes – three, four shapes. They made no noise, they seemed to glide. One of them floundered. I wanted to call out something, but a second shot rang out as Sasha swiftly turned, and another elk – this time I saw him well in the clearing – crashed heavily, head forward.

"What? Two?" I muttered, unable to believe my eyes. "Yes – and a right and left too!" exclaimed Sasha, hugging me round the shoulders. I rarely saw him as happy as he was then.

The beaters came out hurriedly, Sidor trotted up the line

towards us, and the Baron sidled up quite fast, calling out: "Did you get him? They passed me in the thicket. Perhaps if I . . ."

"I got two – right and left!" said Sasha. "The big one first, as he passed following closely behind two cows. The younger one must have been hidden by the old one to begin with. I saw him only as he darted forward after the shot, the cows remaining just a couple of yards behind him."

"Ninety-eight strides to the first," announced Sidor, approaching us and counting loudly. "And some 120 strides to the second, I should think," said Sasha as we walked towards the first elk. What a lovely big animal, antlers spread wide apart, some twelve points on the mighty head.

A photograph was taken by the Baron as the elk were brought home and the Illustrated London News published it in 1912. Like all my photographs, it was lost in the Russian Revolution, but 25 years later my youngest son secured a back number of the magazine and I was able to look at it again and to visualise so vividly the past, and the impressions of this first elk shoot.

KAMENKA

3

ELK

Elk Calling Out of Season

Elk shooting was considered to be one of the finest sports in Northern Russia. We were lucky in always having plenty of elk on our Kamenka estate, and we used to shoot them there through the autumn and early winter.

We usually organised drives, but the sport I really enjoyed was when they were lured during their mating season. This was done by imitating their call.

The mating season begins about the middle of September and lasts until the middle of October, rarely any longer. The best time for luring and for approaching a calling elk is the end of September. During this period the male elk roam over wide areas in search of their mates and also of possible rivals; at this time they are aggressive and can even be dangerous.

I heard of numbers of cases where hunters had been fatally wounded by the forward kick of an attacking elk whose sharp, cleft hoofs must be a formidable weapon for an animal the size of a good horse. As a rule they spend the day feeding quietly in forest glades and in the undergrowth as they are very fond of young aspen shoots. But in the night, especially towards dawn, they start on their quest, wandering about restlessly and uttering their wild, weird, bellowing call which seems to belong to some pre-historic age.

It is by imitating this call that one tries to lure them. Game-keepers – and poachers, of course – have learnt the trick, and generally use a bottle with the bottom knocked out as a megaphone. The difficulty of imitating this call lies in the number of different intonations which obviously vary according to whether it is meant to attract a mate or to challenge a rival.

I was always fascinated by this sport and had observed with keen interest the tactics of one or two of our gamekeepers, expert "callers", when I went with them in search of elk during the long nights of autumn. Such was their art that it never occurred to me that I could ever make use of these observations myself.

But one day I had a very unusual experience which upset all the accepted notions about luring elk. I was in Kamenka during the First World War and was running the forest estate, as my husband and our manager, as well as several foresters, were away in the army. I used to go out daily to various parts of the forests and carried my 12-bore with me, as game was plentiful and provided a pleasant change in the daily menu.

One damp early December day I set out in the morning, planning to visit a distant district which could not be reached on horseback as it lay on the edge of large bogs. It was a murky day but a cold wind rose about noon and the clouds lifted – it looked like clearing up and freezing. Biscuits and some chocolate were my lunch and I trudged happily along the boggy ride towards the more open moor which I meant to cross, when suddenly the call of an elk startled me.

I thought I was dreaming – no elk could call now, at the outbreak of winter and in daytime too. But there it came again, the unmistakable, well-known call. "There's fun", I thought. "I can't approach him on this slushy ground; he'll hear me miles away, but it's stupid to let him go without even trying to get at him!"

I had a couple of bullet cartridges for my shotgun. "Why not try?" I thought. "Besides, this elk must be a queer one anyhow to be calling now, and in broad daylight, too!" Taking a deep breath and using my hands as a megaphone I tried to produce, as well as I could, the yearning elk call, bending towards the ground so as to mellow the sound in case it were too unconvincing.

I think my heart stood still for a few seconds as I uttered this first call and waited, not daring to breathe. And then, suddenly, there came the answer, a very definite and clear reply. The elk had evidently not been frightened off by my attempt to mimic his voice, at any rate not at a considerable distance. Encouraged by this first success I called again – and again the answer came; it was nearer, too.

I called, changing my position so as to make the sound appear more distant. The answer came quite regularly now. It became a proper dialogue. It was fascinating, exciting, time flew.

We called, we talked, we both beat the dry brushwood – I with a stick and the elk obviously with his antlers – we both trampled angrily in the slushy ground and he snorted but I, alas, could not.

Hours passed. The day was waning, the moon rose and the frost came down, sharp, brisk. I had first been wet, then my skirt (I had to wear a skirt so as to appear respectable in the eyes of the country folk) began to freeze until it took the shape of a lampshade, but the elk was still there, near, very near, and most probably puzzled and annoyed by the strange voice of his supposed rival. I peered in vain through the thick undergrowth where a shadow seemed to appear once or twice. I waited for the elk to cross the ride, my gun was ready, cocked, my hands were frozen.

I called and called again, now bending low into the moss trying to disguise at this close range what I felt to be an unconvincing call. The game went on, however; it grew darker, the moon was high, and I could not give up the sport. Finally, the elk grew bored – his opponent was not much of a rival for him, he must have thought, and I heard him stalk away snorting violently, giving angry calls from time to time as if defying or abusing his cowardly rival who would not take up the challenge.

I came back to reality, felt cold, felt the inconvenience of a frozen skirt and the acute sensation of hunger. Reluctantly I turned back and walked along the ride in the direction of home. It was a good two hours' walk and I walked along half conscious of what I was doing. Just following the narrow rides with big patches of moonlight here and there, with the ice cracking under my feet, the stars shining overhead and the voice of the elk still ringing in my ears.

I reached the house at about eight o'clock; the children were in bed, but waiting for me to hear their prayers. Miss Taylor, their nurse, pale and in a flutter, met me on the stairs: she and the servants had thought of sending out a search party for me, and my dog Tiavkin was to guide it.

It was good to be home, warm, to see the boys' sleepy faces and to change into warm and comfortable clothes.

It was particularly pleasant to eat a good dinner and to have a cup of black coffee near the blazing fire – it all seemed unreal after the day's talk with an elk. I really felt proud in my heart of hearts that for several hours on end I had kept an elk at bay, that I could mimic his call with my woman's voice, could pin him to a spot where it had been mere chance – or bad luck – that I had not actually seen him close enough to shoot.

But I never regretted not having shot, for the mere fascination, the fun of the dialogue, had been so great, the voice of the forest, of the elk, seemed to me now to be really part of me and I belonged to it all.

Elk Hunting at Night

An unsuccessful night during the elk-calling season in Russia does not mean much to anyone who has a love for the sport and time to spare. Fortunately I had plenty of both and, I am glad to say, made the best of them. Sidor, the head gamekeeper, and I went out steadily night after night for five days that year – to come home empty-handed every time. It was rather distressing after at least six hours spent in the forests – from about midnight until 6 a.m. We just had no luck. One day our lantern, left at the crossing of two rides, fell on its side after we had gone and the smell of the spilt paraffin was enough to send any elk away for miles. Another night an elk began to answer our call but was lured away by other elk and we could hear them in the distance. Anyhow, there we were, empty-handed, and I felt rather ashamed as my little sons looked at me enquiringly when I came down to breakfast with no story about elk. Thus, on the sixth night I decided not to go out, hoping to break the streak of bad luck.

However, at about 11 p.m., as I was still reading in my study, I heard the well-known knock on my window. Sidor was there.

"The weather is too good, my lady, it would be a sin to miss a night like this. Look at the moon." Indeed, the moon was brilliant, and there was no cloud, not a breath of wind; only clear fresh air with the promise of a frost before dawn. I was soon ready and we started. No hurricane lamp was needed this time. It was one of those wonderful northern September nights, light, silent, so clear and starlit that one could see the relief of trees and bushes as if it were daylight. It was easy walking and we soon reached the haunts of the elk. We arrived there at 2 a.m. and Sidor began calling. He had learnt a lot from the elk of our first night and his call sounded now more convincing than ever, deep, bellowing, angry and with the flourish of the dying sigh at the end. I think he was thrilled by it himself and the transparent air seemed to carry the sound in waves through the low forests and across the wide moors. It was still night, but the faint grey tint of the coming dawn penetrated the forest from above and mingled with the moonlight. About twenty minutes after our start we heart a distant short, rather barking, answer. "An old male," whispered Sidor, "we must be very careful – they are sharp." I knew well enough that we had to be cautious and my hands turned the gun into a handy position – much too early of course. How clumsy and heavy one always feels at such moments when everything depends upon one's movements!

Sidor called again and immediately the same angry barking answered, "He's coming," muttered Sidor, "we shall have to tease him until it's light enough to shoot." We stood still waiting; it was best not to call too often. Soon there came the impatient bark again. The conversation had to be kept up for a while with great care and certainly with skill on the part of Sidor. The light was coming now, the frost too. My hand was chilled grabbing the barrel of the gun and my feet numb from standing in the slushy ground. And still the game went on – a call, an answer; and then a repeated angry bark getting more and more impatient. It was time to start the approach tactics and I agreed with Sidor to take up my position about 20 yards forward behind a group of small fir trees, while he would retreat calling. As soon as Sidor started breaking dry branches by beating them down with a stick in imitation of an angry elk's swish with the antlers, I advanced as heavily as I could towards the approaching elk. The angry reply came faster now. My post was good, the dark firs hid my darkish suit better than the brushwood with the light autumn tints, I stood still, listening intently, and tried to see through the silvery grey surroundings.

A light mist was rising, and the forest was becoming veiled and white, the mist mingling with the light of dawn and the still shining moonlight. It was very cold now, with white frost settling on the long moor grass, the bushes and the trees. Looking over my shoulder I could see Sidor crouching on the ground giving his low muffled call. Then, in front of me and this time very close, there came the bark, a heavy trampling in the slushy ground, and the breaking of dead wood. Suddenly something moved behind the screen of brushwood – a large shadow, something I knew to be the elk. Would he come closer? Would he follow the retreating Sidor and pass me in his pursuit?

The grey shadow vanished. Had he gone? Had he guessed my presence? Then a crushing of twigs in front of me, some thirty yards away, and the magnificent head with silvery shining antlers thrown back appeared suddenly out of a young aspen thicket. I felt it more than I saw it; his eyes, small as they were, seemed to pierce the faint, grey mist – a slight snort reached my ear, the steam of breath rose in the frosty air. He was a beauty – all silvery now in the grey dawn, the slight frost covering him, the ground, the thicket, the hanging cobwebs. He was too beautiful to shoot – but I was young – and Sidor had worked so well. I levelled the gun, my aim was the neck just above the shoulder, which was all that I could see clearly, except the head. I heard the shot, and staggered back as I always did when using my husband's gun, and the elk crashed among the young aspen.

He was a large 10-pointer; a dark-brown, stilted-legged bull. Sidor admired him, at the same time congratulating me and recalling every detail of the approach. But for me this was not the proud silvery animal I had seen – that one must have escaped – for he was too beautiful to have died.

Many years have gone by and I always remember him as my "silver elk" embodying the beauty of a northern September night and that of our great forests.

Elk Tracking

For years, since my childhood, I had heard fantastic stories about the great art of tracking game as practised by certain hunters of North-Western Russia, more exactly by the "Pskovichi" – men from the province of Pskov, South of Petersburg. The art of the Pskovichi seemed to me the utmost perfection of sport as it was linked with the complete understanding of nature and animal life. With eager interest I listened to all stories about these men and always hoped to see them at work someday. As gamekeepers they were highly appreciated but seemed none too willing to leave their native forests. Time passed, I married a man as keen on shooting as I was, although I had to admit that my passion did not go as far as his, for he could read for days on end volumes and volumes of the well-known sportive review called *Pritoda i Okhota*, which accumulated on his table and around his armchair in impressive numbers. I was more choosy and picked out my Pskovichi stories; I found that they took enough of my time anyhow.

Well supplied with knowledge from these and other books and with my own practical experience after several years of shooting in our forests of the Petersburg province, I only waited for an opportunity to try my hand at the art of tracking game myself. The idea of doing this independently, without making use of my own gamekeepers, attracted me a lot, but it was not easy for a woman, and for the owner of the place too, to start such a novel thing – as tracking! Who had ever heard of it? Not a woman's job! Too ridiculous! And I was coward enough to fear this "ridiculous". After all, I was a remnant of very Victorian days and of Edwardian education – this is my excuse.

But with the outbreak of the war, the absence of my husband, who was with the forces, and the shortage of gamekeepers and men on the estate in general, many things had to change, and I had and could do a lot of things on my own. I had to undertake work for which a woman of my class had not been exactly prepared. Our estate manager too had to go soon after the outbreak of the war and I took over the management of our estate, so the country folk soon got used to seeing me riding through the forests, checking up on the work there, or driving my small sledge when walking on skis was too tiring.

Thus, I set out on skis one dull wintry morning to have a look at some distant district where felling was to start after Christmas. As usual I took my shotgun with me, slipping some bullet cartridges loose in my pocket. Chocolate and a few biscuits were to be my lunch as I could not be back in time and preferred the children to have their meal without me, as their nurse, Miss Taylor, did not like to have their timetable upset. After about two miles on the road with the skis trailing behind me, I turned right along a ride and slipped on the skis. By the way, our forest skis had leather loops for the tip of the foot and were slipped on like a bedroom slipper, without being fixed to the boot as the mountain skis are. The idea was that in the forests we were constantly obliged to slip them off in order to climb over fallen tree trunks or to make our way through brushwood where skis would have only delayed us and got entangled.

Very soon I came across the marks of two or three elk; one of these left a particularly large imprint on the soft snow. It looked to me, however, that the animals had passed here in the night, as the snow on the edge of the marks looked already crumbly and glassy. Not paying much attention to these marks I went on thinking of the object of my walk – the "delianka" or felling district to be verified. How conscientious one can be when young and when entrusted suddenly with a big and unknown task! Besides, this feeling of responsibility and duty seems to have weighed very heavily upon those who have had the privilege of enjoying a good late-Victorian education (perhaps a questionable privilege for those who were later obliged to make their own way in life in entirely new and very non-Victorian conditions).

As I went on, the tracks crossed my way again and again, getting more numerous. At least five or six animals must have been here. I reached the "delianka" all right and walked carefully around it to make sure of what was to be done before the felling began. And the tracks, very fresh now and very numerous, crossed and re-crossed within this district, attracting my attention, distracting me from my work. My consolation was that my husband had often abandoned his task to check up on tracks – and in spite of it things had gone on all right. Soon the tracks were making such a lively pattern on the snow that I could not help trying to read

them. Away flew all my good intentions of hard work, my sense
of duty. Footprints and more of them, scores and in all varieties,
large and small, narrow and wide, which meant male and female
elk and their calves, were puzzling me now. Really there must
have been a sort of great family gathering last night and I got so
interested in them that nothing else seemed to exist on earth: just
reading these marks, seeing where they lead to, where the larger
bulls are and whether there would be any chance of approaching
them. Concentrating all my attention on this new sport of reading,
I followed the main track first, trying to make out the individual
marks from the bull. It was not an easy job: footprints walked
off only to join the main stream a couple of yards further; others
seemed to join the rest from the outside or to go off for good.
Time flew, I walked slowly, carefully marking the larger imprints
at all crossings of the different rides. Feeling somewhat hungry
and very hot I looked at my watch – three o'clock! Can it be so
late? Already? It will soon be dark and I simply must find the big
bulls of the herd, make out their individual tracks and try to see
where they are driving the lot. Reading soon became easier: I got
used to the various prints and knew quite well that this must be
the eldest bull with his wide and deep imprint, and this must be
his rival, as he never walks too closely to the grandfather, and
this is the frolicking nephew who goes off on a spree but joins
up with the lot pretty quickly because he must be a Don Juan, I
assumed, and can't keep away for too long a time from the society
of charming and attractive ladies. And here is the philosopher (if
there are any among elk?), for he keeps aside from the rest but
has not the courage of his convictions and cannot go quite on
his own, following his ideals and thoughts. In fact, I began to
visualise them all and made myself a good picture of the party,
which consisted of some 17 to 20 elk altogether. However, it
began to get colder and darker, I realised that the house was far
away and that I had to start on my way home if I wanted to
get there before night. Reluctantly I decided to go, noting again
the various crossing of rides, making darts on the snow to mark
the general trend or direction followed by the herd. The weather
did not look like changing and there were all chances that the
elk would not change their feeding places over night as I had

not, I hoped, frightened them today. Hopes of a good day's work tomorrow cheered me.

As I skied home between the double wall of high fir trees in the gathering dark of the early winter day I suddenly realised that the work I had been doing all these hours must be on the lines of the work carried out by the Pskovichi; that subconsciously I had been applying my own experiences and all I had learnt from my husband and my gamekeepers with the recollections of my reading. This idea thrilled me; I simply must carry out my task to the end and corner my elk tomorrow; drive them to the point where I can have a chance of a shot at the big males. This prospect thrilled me and I never noticed how I finally reached home in utter darkness – and exhausted.

But once in my study, how my conscience troubled me! Where was my "delianka"? Where the figures I proposed to give to Ivan Pavlov, the forester of that district? And what about my trip to Vassilievskoe tomorrow, the village some three miles away where the priest wanted my advice (which I obviously could give only in vague grunts) about a site for the new village hall? Where are all these duties when I even forget that my boys had been waiting in vain for their hour of games and fairy tales before their bedtime? How easily the thought of duties flies out of one's head! I feel repentant, sorry – but the elk must be found tomorrow – they won't wait.

Tomorrow arrived quickly enough – a grey and quiet day, much to my relief. An early breakfast when the boys were still dressing and I went off with gun and skis leaving Tiavkin, my devoted Samoyed, well locked up in the house, for he would spoil my game – in this particular case. An hour and a half later I was in the forest where the tracks had been last marked by me in the evening. Nothing fresh for a couple of yards; then the marks of the old man with a couple of ladies crossing the ride leisurely. Eagerly I picked them up, cautiously following them into the thicket, but soon retraced my steps as I could not see any distance and could only frighten the animals who may be not so far away, the marks being very fresh. Would this be the direction taken by the whole herd? To judge by the slight wind that had risen in the morning, it could be so, but I was anxious to check up on my supposition by following some other tracks. A few yards further the traces of another group going in the same direction crossed my way. This is lucky, I thought, as the direction does lead towards the big moor and before that are generally spaces with sparse growth where there would be a chance of seeing the elk at some distance without running into them, as would be the case in the brushwood. It seemed to be too good to be true. And then came large, splashing traces of several elk, long strides, hurried steps, sprays of snow! Had I really frightened them? I was terrified. Had I taken up the track too closely? Were they now on the go for good and would the other groups join them in the flight? All these thoughts crossed my mind in rapid succession. I tried to make up my mind whether I should or should not go on with my quest. The pale wintry sun came out now somehow cheering me in my depression. I'll try to carry on as best I can, perhaps . . .

Somewhat further on the ride, very narrow here, a mere line, I came across another track, the lonely philosopher's, I thought, and he did not seem to be upset, sedate big strides, some nibbling of aspen shoots, a picture of peaceful feeding. How relieved I felt; perhaps the fleeing ones were only having some exercise, perhaps they were the one ones having a game? Soon loops of tracks crossed and re-crossed the ride, the general tendency was leaning towards the bog or perhaps now more towards the large aspen contingents where the undergrowth makes further tracking impossible, for the elk will probably settle there for the night. I must try to exert some pressure to get them towards the bog. Retracing my steps I took a cross line – here two or three of the younger lot seemed to have been across but were not followed by any of the large animals. Something must be done to prevent the old ones from following; I took my scarf and hung it well in sight on the right. Cautiously hurrying on along the same line I soon discarded one glove, then the other, hanging them also well in open spaces. This should frighten the animals off if they press against this line. Another lot re-crossed into the part where I expected the main herd to be – they were the same young ones who had gone to the right. All right, I thought, they don't seem too intent yet on the aspen forest, and to my left the skyline began to clear – surely the approaches of the bog. And then my ride opened onto a large glade at the other end of which I could already see the whiteness of the bog. The elk must be near the glade where the young aspen trees grow fast with juicy young shoots! How to drive the lot along the glade towards the clearer spaces – not to frighten them? No time to reflect over this problem as the daylight would not last too long. I'll try to creep as cautiously as I can, under the cover of the first bushes skirting the glade, it was my only chance. How I walked, how I sneaked my way from bush to bush, leaving here my jacket, there my cap, I cannot remember. How long it took me, I don't know – it obviously seemed to last hours and hours. I held my breath, listening for even the smallest noise, for every crack of a twig, and once or twice my heart stood still when the dull sound of a falling lump of snow resounded to me like a gunshot. Then I realised, there was no snow on the bushes, some was lying on the thick branches of lonely fir trees and a bird or a squirrel must have made it drop. On I went, the longed-for sparsely wooded space was here, some twenty yards from me, the glade was ending in with a narrow strip of brushwood closing it in from the bog – and then I heard, distinctly, clearly, the shuffling sound of elk on the go. Crouching down behind a thick-ish bush, the gun ready in hand – I waited. An elk cow stepped out of the thicket with the calf at her side – sniffed round indifferently, ears flopping and nearly covering her eyes – the next, another cow, apparently quiet and undisturbed, sniffing the air too – were they sent out to spy the land, as gamekeepers always assured me was their job? Were they cautious because they had come across some of my things along the line? I could not tell, but felt the strain of the moment, for the old bulls must follow, must be near. And then one of them really came out, suddenly, preceded by another cow. He stopped, his head high, his nostrils wide open – what a lovely picture! My shot fell – and so did the bull – it was an easy shot for he stood there on the open. There was a stampede towards the bog and back into the forest. I could not see anything clearly anymore – it was such a grand feeling to have achieved my goal after these two days of heavy work. And I knew now that I could do the job of a Pskovich – at least I have done it once!

4

LYNX

What Ought to Have Been My First Lynx

In 1908 I had never yet seen a lynx – except of course in pictures and even then not very frequently. We had two or three carpets made of lynx furs covering sofas or lying on the floor under writing tables or in front of the fire. Still, I could not picture our snow-bound northern forests with some tiger-like animal wandering there and being quite at home in this cold and frost. For the lynx is so much larger than a wild cat – as it is often described in zoological books – and with its rather large head and ferocious expression it reminds one more of a leopard or jaguar than of a cat. At least this is how I pictured this new animal as I stood alone on the stand, gun in hand, and the injunctions of my husband still ringing in my ears: "Mind you don't move and keep your eyes well open – the lynx is a cunning animal and very difficult to see." So I stood there, knee-deep in the snow. I was standing on my skis but they had sunk so deep into the thick soft snow that I felt as if I weighed tons and tons.

The snow had been falling for a good twenty-four hours without stopping and the clouds, as if tired of shedding and shedding it, were scarcely moving now, hanging low over the land. The overburdened forests were stooping under the weight of masses of fresh snow. Not a breath of wind, perfect and complete silence in the grey-white frosty air. Large trees, sparse undergrowth, quaint rounded white shapes – probably overturned tree-trunks – all round me. The smallest twig carried a load of snow, willow bushes and young fir trees were bent like arches, both ends buried in it.

I will see the snow fall off any of these twigs if the lynx touches one – it will be a warning, I thought, and felt reassured about not missing it. In front of me, at my very feet, a ditch-like path running from right to left had been trodden down by the gamekeepers and beaters, all on skis, as they had passed me to take up their positions all along the beat. We were three guns: I was the left flank one, my brother came next, then my husband. A score of yards to my left the line of red flags began enveloping this side of the beat.

I was listening – not a sound, only the blood in my ears thumping, probably from excitement, perhaps from the quick walk on skis, as we had to go a good long distance from the road where the sledges remained. It was a dark and dull day in midwinter and we had no time to lose before dusk set in.

Suddenly a signal, the muffled noise of the beaters, their shouts rising in front of me as if they came out of the ground, so dull, so soundless in this mass of snow. My gun ready, finger near the trigger, I stood motionless, afraid to breathe, just turning my eyes slowly right and left. Nearer and nearer came the beaters, I could hear their regular howls and yells, they must have come across the fresh tracks of the lynx; they shouted with excitement, probably more tracks in front of me somewhere close by. I don't know how long it lasted, but the forest remained motionless, the cushions of snow undisturbed on even the smallest twig. Not a movement, not the faintest shadow.

There were the beaters. I saw them all covered with snow, caps, beards, eyebrows, shoulders, all white, only their faces red and shining, steaming from the hard walk – and nothing, not a shot.

"Where can the beasts have gone to?" I wonder.

From the left suddenly the call: "Here it was, there are the fresh tracks – and what a bound across the path!"

I am aghast – Ivan Ivanovich, the oldest gamekeeper, stands there, some twenty-five yards from me, his gun on his shoulder, bending his long gaunt figure to look closer at the tracks to which he points with a long stick. "Yes, they passed both here, track in track, the second gave a slightly shorter bound . . ."

My brother is looking at me. "What, did you not see them? Impossible . . . only twenty-five yards at the most," he says, with a rather indignant look on his face.

I feel ashamed, dreadfully ashamed. How could I miss them? I looked so intently, so attentively all the time, I am sure nothing moved anywhere and the snow had remained untouched, unshaken on all trees and branches I could see. Impossible. I go up to Ivan Ivanovich. No doubt; there they are the fresh powdery tracks, and what a leap across the suspicious path! I turn back to my stand. Could I see them from there? Had I really clean missed them with my eyes?

My husband has joined us now, he stands up on the exact spot where I stood, looks critically at the place where the lynxes crossed; "Well, there is the bend of the path, also that mound of snow – but perhaps if you had craned your neck – or been six-foot-two – you might have seen them."

What a relief – it was not altogether my fault as I am very far from six-foot-two and all neck craning could not have brought me much nearer to it. Still, from that day on I dreaded the news of "lynxes in the beat" and always felt that I should have had eyes all round my head for this shooting. Once I did break this nasty spell and, having got one lynx, began to have more confidence in my capacity to detect them. But it is true that lynxes are as lithe and cunning in their movements as any cat, and suspecting danger they will crawl on their stomach, making a regular furrow in the snow and avoiding in the most skilful manner any bush or twig which might betray their presence by shedding its burden of snow.

A Family of Lynx

In Northern Russia, February is the month of violent snowstorms, sharp frosts and occasional mild and sunny days. The winter is anxious to display all its strength and power before giving way to spring – so goes a popular saying in these parts of the country. The same saying can, often enough, be applied to the month of March, but the piercing February winds are more biting and the sunny days more rare.

On one of these rare sunny days following a series of blinding snowstorms the gamekeeper Sidor came home after his morning round and reported that he had tracked a family of lynxes in one of his beats, apparently six of them. This sounded too good to be true, but he was quite positive about it, having carefully checked all the tracks. It is rare to come across more than a couple of full-grown lynx together; frequently you may find the mother with small cubs, three or rarely four. But the old father lynx objects to the noise of the cubs and prefers to stay some distance from them, a little out of earshot.

It was therefore an exceptionally lucky find to have them all together in one beat. We had a hurried lunch and set off in four sledges – my brother, my husband and myself being the only three guns that day. Sidor followed with our skis and the reels of red rags for partly encircling the beat; then followed two sledges with some of the more experienced beaters, the others being recruited by another gamekeeper from the nearest village. We were on the stands after a tiring ski run from the road where the sledges had to be left. My brother drew the best stand – the middle one – Sidor shook his head with concern, as he did not consider my brother a good shot – and not entirely without reason either.

The beat was large and we, the guns, were further apart from each other than usual. To my right I could see the trees thinning into sparse growth on the edge of the great moors which stretched out for miles to the north; to my left, towards my brother, a narrow strip of denser growth of fir tree reached to within a few yards of the narrow ride along which we stood. Sidor had nodded towards this strip as we moved silently to our positions and I understood that the lynx would probably take that way within easy range of my brother's gun. His luck, I thought, as he had never shot a lynx yet. I was glad of the good opportunity before him.

It was quiet and not cold; I could easily crane my neck to have a good look round and need not draw it back into the thick white muffler (the Russian *bashlyk*) in which I warmed my freezing chin. My usual anxiety about missing or not spying the lynx in time had vanished as there was little chance of anything coming my way. Still, one never knows, I thought, remembering the size of the family.

The beat started, the usual distant rumour growing louder and louder, then separate voices and familiar shouts of the beaters, the usual tension of the nerves and cautious glances right and left – "only not to let one slip through unnoticed" was my constant preoccupation.

Then, suddenly, a shot to my left – my brother evidently – and immediately a second shot. "Two already" was my natural conclusion, and I looked carefully to my left expecting some members of the lynx family to dart across the ride. Then two more shots in rapid succession – "Well, he is lucky!" The shouts of the bearers grow louder – then one shot again, my brother's, and yet another. A few seconds later a more distant, fainter shot. This really is too much – he has had six shots – he must have had the whole family there – real beginner's luck – and I am just a little envious for my husband as he is a keen shot and would have liked to get a fine old lynx. The shouts are frantic now, calls of "here they were! they passed there – a real herd!" come from the thicket. Sidor appears on the ride and runs towards my brother, the beaters are within a few yards of me – they are all out now for certain. I rush off towards my brother to see the bag.

"How many? Where are they?" I call to him.

But he is talking excitedly, gesticulating, pointing constantly towards the same spot in front of his stand. My husband, Sidor and the other gamekeepers listen, shrug their shoulders, and from their looks I guess that something has gone wrong.

"Well, what's happened?" I ask, coming nearer.

"You see they all come straight out at me, all five of them!" says my brother with animation.

"All right – but how many have you got?"

"Not one – no not one!"

"What? Not a single one? But that's impossible!"

My brother looks indignant. "The first came there – stopped, apparently to look at me, so I shot straight at him, aiming at his head, he jerked, scowled and meowed loudly, bouncing back into the thicket. Then another one, also a young one, I think, looked at me from the same spot and I shot at him – he too scowled and meowed and was away. I had just time to reload my gun when two more came, they did the same thing – it was so funny because I already expected them and waited for the meow – they did not seem to mind my shots."

"I don't wonder!" put in my husband with a sour smile.

45

"Well, I shot at them right enough and then came the mother – at least I think it was her – and she too stopped to look at me and had a long look, for I had time to aim better – but she also turned away in spite of my shot and with a meow too – a deeper one, another tone."

"So she even got an extra shot then?" I put in.

"No, she got two," said my husband, "and I had the last shot – at the old man – and got him. A fine spotted one as big as a calf!"

Sidor and another gamekeeper came now carrying the old lynx between them, a real beauty, very large and perfectly marked.

"Did yours meow too?" asked my brother.

"No, they only meow at those who miss," answered my husband.

I was sorry for my brother but fortunately he did not seem to mind the mishap. "They did look so amusing as they meowed," he kept on repeating, "and their faces twisted into a ferocious scowl."

Poor Sidor did not see the joke, though, and I could hear him muttering to himself, "Such an opportunity happens once in one's lifetime and I'll never get such a beat again!"

My consolation was that none of the meowing family had been hit as there was not a drop of blood on the snow where they had turned back. Perhaps this experience will make them less afraid of human beings in the future, I thought, with a rather greedy feeling at the back of my mind.

The Baby Lynx

The mother lynx must be a very clever mother, for it is extremely rare to come across her with a very young baby. Obviously they know well how to hide and I assume that they even take the baby up a tree, although it is only in exceptional cases that one finds a climbing lynx. Sometimes they take refuge in the trees when they are wounded – at least this is what used to be said by hunters who had had quite a bit of experience with these animals.

One day, shortly before Christmas, I think, we set out in search of a lynx which had been surrounded in a far-off beat and on very unsatisfactory snow: old snow which had been thawing slightly and on which the tracks showed very poorly. The gamekeeper had warned us that there was one animal with perhaps a small baby, but he was not certain himself. It was a dark, dull afternoon with more thaw in the air. The beaters made some mistake and one flank came out earlier than the other: we were only two guns on a very long line – altogether things did not seem to go well.

"Where is the lynx?" we asked each other when we all met on the line. There were no tracks near us, none seen by the gamekeepers. A delayed beater, a former poacher who had settled down now as a worthy farmer, came with the news that he had found fresh tracks and that they led into the fir thicket and disappeared there. He was positive that the animal had climbed a tree. We surrounded the thicket, then went through it with shouts and beating of bushes, but not a sign of life to be seen. It was dusk already and we were giving up all hopes of finding our lynx that day when suddenly my husband raised his gun, shot, and some fifty yards from us the dull thud of a falling body could be heard. We rushed there and found a pale-tinted lynx lying on the ground. As the beaters were crowding round to have a look at it, one of them, pushing his way through a cluster of small fir trees, nearly stepped on a small baby lynx crouching there. We soon got hold of it in spite of the furious spitting, mauling and scratching, wrapped it up in the bundle of red rags used for encircling the beat, and carried it to the sledges.

It was a real beauty – pale cream fur with a white tummy and paws, large green eyes, black tips on its ears and a funny little tassel of black fur at the end of its stumpy tail. It was as large as a big cat, higher on its legs but a little shorter in length.

I was terribly sorry for the little animal and decided to do all I could for it. There was no question of letting it free as it was too small yet to survive in the forest and would certainly have died of hunger. As we drove home I tried to pat its head as I held it closely, wrapped up so its angry paws were safely hidden, but the furious look I got, the ferocious meow and scowl was so impressive that I refrained from further attempts to sooth it.

Once home, the problem of feeding had to be solved. We tried in vain to push its nose into a saucer with tepid and sweetened milk – the little animal spat furiously and only got excited. We got him a baby's bottle from the village but the same spitting and fighting thwarted all our efforts. I was absolutely at a loss and could not think of the lonely little animal dying of hunger. Something had to be done.

Late that evening as I came to check on the baby lynx in the deep box in which we had prepared a cosy bed for it, I noticed how it had dug its nose into the old bit of fur that I had put there to keep it warm. This gave me the idea of wrapping up the milk bottle into a fur – and better still, into one of the lynx furs we had as carpets. Then and there we arranged a furry bottle and I cautiously put it down in the box right against the animal's nose. It was sleepy, apparently, and did not jump up in a fury, but sniffed, sniffed again, put its nose into the fur and, as I raised the bottle slightly to its mouth, the little animal suddenly pounced upon it and began to suck with avidity, gulping, gurgling, but going on. It was a relief and a joy, and when I went to bed an hour later after having tucked in the sleeping baby with a nice round tummy, I felt happy to think that at least it was quite satisfied.

From that first successful feeding we never had any more difficulties with it and it took its bottle with evident pleasure, though always making a scowling face when we first approached it. Weeks and weeks later we began to give it some meat, to which it took eagerly, but we never could make it eat bread or biscuits, except soaked in milk or meat juice.

We had hoped to be able to keep the lynx in the house, but it seemed impossible to train it in any way: it simply remained a wild forest animal and did not react to any of our efforts to make it obey. It did not show any sign of recognising its name "Rysik", and it did not manifest any more sympathy towards the person who fed it than to any one else in the house. I was obliged to keep it in a sort of kennel, or rather a small hut built for it in a grove of pine trees in the park on the shores of the brook. We could see it from the windows of the house as it played with fur cones just as a cat plays with a mouse.

Rysik had grown a lot and towards the end of the summer he was as tall as a good-sized Airedale terrier. His coat was smooth but not thick, evidently his summer coat still, his paws large and his claws impressive. Only a few people ventured to come near him and I certainly discouraged strangers from approaching Rysik, he looked too serious and attentive to be safe. Unfortunately we had to keep him on a long chain, for although we did not fear his attacking people, there was absolutely no doubt that he would go for the hens, chicks, ducks or geese. It was enough to see from a distance how he watched, intently, passionately, all the movements of the ducks and geese on the brook. The sudden darts he made for them were a test to the chain, and more than once I had to see that it was fastened more securely to the trunk of the old fir tree or that the ring in his collar was in order. No enclosure would have kept it back – except perhaps very tall and smooth iron bars – but we could not have these, far away as we were in the country.

So Rysik lived on, looking a real beauty now with a spotty coat getting nice and thick now towards winter and evidently not too unhappy in his private little park. The only sign of his being tired of captivity was that he often walked up and down as far as his long chain would allow it, rather in the way you see tigers and lions do in their cages in the zoo. But I did not like to see this walking up and down and did not quite know what to do with Rysik. He knew me well enough, at least I could come near and pat him now, and he seldom scowled or spat. But somehow I felt wrong keeping him chained. To let him free would seem wrong too, as lynxes are considered beasts of prey since they destroy game. Fortunately Rysik found himself the proper solution.

One cold and quiet moonlight night in late autumn, it must have been the beginning of November, I heard the dogs barking and went out on the doorstep to whistle to them. They came back eagerly, there was apparently nothing unusual outside, perhaps a village cat roaming near the kennels. And in the morning, there was no Rysik, a broken collar tied to the chain.

We never saw him again, and we never shot one that was as beautifully marked as he was, and that was a relief to me, as I could not bear the idea of Rysik being hit. I hope he found his way to some far-off forest and lived his own independent life there without too much hatred for mankind.

5

BEARS

Encounters with Bears in the North

Bears were not as numerous anymore even in 1910 as they used to be in former days, but they were still a familiar wild animal and one that was rather liked – from a distance though – and not hated as the wolf. To shoot a bear was still considered the height of a sportsman's luck and to be invited to a bear shoot was always regarded as a favour.

The brown bear of Northern Russia and Siberia is an exclusively forest animal, keeping only to large stretches of forests where he can roam about for miles and miles without coming across human beings; where villages and fields are scarce, like islands in a sea of trees. This does not mean, however, that the bear always keeps away from human dwellings; there are certain times of the year when he rather likes to roam near fields and meadows. Towards autumn, for instance, when he seems to have a particularly good appetite, probably laying in the supply of fat which keeps him warm during the winter sleep. The villagers do fear him for then for he is apt to lay his paw on the young stock and sheep grazing on the forest glades, but I have never heard of bears attacking men, except in self-defence when already wounded. Then, of course, he is a terrible animal, baffling by the rapidity of his movements and the incredible strength of his paws: I have seen a young birch, some twenty years old or more, fly into bits as if under the blows of a sharp axe when a wounded bear stood up on his hind legs and went for it mistaking it for his enemy, the man who had wounded him in the head.

It seems strange that an animal with whom nature has supplied such impressive teeth and claws finds particular taste in dainty food like honey, wild berries of all kinds and oats. More than once we came across holes dug out under old roots with wild honey combs scattered about – and very evident signs of the bear's paws having done the digging. In other places one could see how he had combed bilberries off the low bushes, broken shoots of wild raspberries which grow in masses in these northern forests, or bent to the ground, if not broken, young mountain ashes in order to pluck the berries of which the bear is apparently very fond. It is quite wrong to think that the bear won't touch a dead animal, as is often told – on the contrary, he rather likes the game to be a little "high", and when we wanted to make sure that a bear was roaming in certain parts of our forests we put out in distant, secluded places the carcass of an old horse and if a bear was near he came back to his meals quite regularly, even though the approach of the spot was not very pleasant for humans. Such delicacies as dead horses were put out for the bears in September and October so as to attract them to certain districts and to entice them to remain there for their winter sleep. "Border" bears, as we called those we supposed to dwell in our and in the neighbour's forests, had a very good time in autumn as both sides tried to attract them, and the more "high" the meal, the greater was the chance of having the bear stay on that side. The competition between the gamekeepers was great and their ideas as to what the bear likes or dislikes were very definite. There were gamekeepers specialising in bear hunting, tracking, organising the shoots, finding their lairs under the snow, distorting their tracks and, among others, specialising in bringing up bear cubs. These men got a better salary than the others and were not easy to get.

But I return to the true experience I once had with my son. It was in early August, I think. I took out my eldest boy, then aged nine, for a stroll in the forest in search of squirrels for him as he had a 22 Winchester rifle, and young heather cocks for myself. My pointer, Sport, was with us. When we came to a ride between the old forest and the thicket of young fir trees, birches and aspens I sent Sport into the thicket. He disappeared there but soon dashed back whining, trembling and seeking refuge at my feet. I sent him in again, he disappeared for only a second and reappeared with the same whining and trembling. Evidently there was something that had really frightened Sport, I could not quite imagine what, as we were not very far from the fields and home. As I tried to soothe Sport my son suddenly called out to me: "Look here, Mother, what strange big paw marks on the clay! Look there, right under the ash tree."

Surely enough, on the damp clay of the ditch running along the ride and recently cleaned, there were clearly marked footprints of a bear, not a big one, as my hand more or less covered the footprint. A few stray berries of the mountain ash lay scattered on the ground and the lower branches of the young tree hung limp, half broken.

"It is a bear – he must be in this small bit of thicket," I said. "We'll try to cut his way back to the big forest. Stand still here and keep your gun ready – don't move on any account – and shoot only if the bear passes there – and showing you his side – don't shoot if he faces you – never."

The boy was rather overawed and nodded silently. I put him behind a very large tree trunk and pointed at the place – at a good distance – where he would be allowed to shoot. "If he comes nearer – don't shoot, don't move – look at him and enjoy it."

With these words and whistling slightly for Sport to follow me, I set off at a trot on the soft meadow grass round the thicket. I ran as fast as I could, but the thicket stretched out quite a bit and when I reached the other end of it and the ditch on the edge of the big forest, I had the disappointment – and the satisfaction – of seeing the black form of a bear leap across the ditch, too far for my boy to be able to shoot. I must say, I was quite glad that the bear went without a shot, for, as I ran round the thicket the thought had crossed my mind that it may not have been exactly wise to leave the boy – so young – all alone to face the possibility of quite serious danger.

We soon met; the boy was delighted to have had this chance of catching sight of the bear and certainly had not thought of any possible danger.

"Would you have shot if he had come out of the thicket a little nearer?" I asked him as we were walking home discussing the excitement of the day.

"No, you said not to – and you know best."

I was pleased with the confidence he had in my knowledge, but much more pleased to see how happy he was to have had this experience and proud to have been the first to have seen the footprints on the damp clay.

* * *

It was a very warm summer in our northern forests near Petersburg. My little boys, then aged eight, six and three, spent the greater part of the day playing in an abandoned sandpit at the very edge of the large pine and fir tree forest which stretched for miles on end. The sandpit was on the top of a small hill and from the drawing room windows I could see the little figures of the children climbing up and rolling down, digging, building sandcastles and their faithful nurse Miss Taylor sitting on the green bank with her needlework and perhaps a basket of fruit. When not paddling in the brook the boys were in their favourite sandpit and in the hay barn next to it. The slopes of the hillock were ploughed and that year we had a particularly good crop of oats there.

When the time came to harvest the oats the boys found great fascination in following the work of the horse-drawn mower. And then one day, I heard a big discussion going on as the boys were coming home for tea along the narrow path leading down the hillock. The two big boys were pleading for something and Miss Taylor was refusing energetically – that much I could make out as I watched them from the garden. "Please, please!" I could hear the two big boys repeat time after time. "No – no . . ." and expressive shaking of the head on the part of Miss Taylor. What was it all about? The boys rushed into the dining room.

"Mother, Mother, we have seen the bed of a bear . . ."

"Of our bear, our bear of the sandpit!"

I could not make out what it all meant and what bear they had in the sandpit. Miss Taylor managed at last to put in her word. Apparently the mowers in cutting the corner of the field nearest to the sandpit came across a bear's lair, his summer resting place, where he had evidently spent many a pleasant hour eating the oats off the stalks – and that some thirty yards from the sandpit.

"You must see the bed he has made for himself!" said one of the boys, "All nice and soft moss he dragged from the forest – you can see the path he made for himself, quite a big path too."

"And the oats he has been eating, all round his bed," put in the other boy.

"And he was rolling round and round to get more and more oats," said the third.

"And to think that we were sitting there all these weeks, day after day, with the children running about!" said Miss Taylor, shuddering with terror at the thought of what might have happened. "No playing in the sandpit anymore – this is what I am telling the boys now," she added very firmly.

This made me smile – I could not persuade her right then that there was no danger any more since the oats were cut and food and shelter could not be found there anymore. But after tea we did go there with the boys to have a good look at the place and I came to the conclusion that a bear knows how to make himself comfortable and that he prefers oats to little boys. Had he been at all interested in human beings he would have had a grand chance. The place he had chosen and snuggily arranged with a thick bedding of moss, "his bedroom" as the boys called it, was really only a few yards from the castles and dug-outs adorning the sandpit and the forest for safe escape was also but a few yards to the north. The quantity of oats the bear had apparently stripped into his open front paws between his toes was very impressive too.

The boys were delighted about it all, but Miss Taylor refused to go back to the sandpit and as the bad weather set in soon, the question was dropped anyhow. I have a suspicion that the two younger boys secretly agreed with their nurse but were not quite courageous enough to admit it before their big brother, who was only too thrilled to have been thus in real danger and who insisted on going to watch and even to stalk the bear. I had to put my foot down here and to make him promise not to go to the sandpit with his little Winchester rifle when he was out on one of his "shooting expeditions", as he called his stalking of rats, squirrels or even mice on the farm and in the garden. I think he had some difficulty in keeping to his promise but did stick to it in spite of the great temptation.

* * *

I met or rather came across bears by chance only twice, and both times I did not really see them well. One day towards the end of August I had to ride to a distant part of the forest where felling was going to start in September. It was a very warm day and as there was neither a road nor a path leading to the place, I followed the edge of a brook where the horse could pick its way more easily. The valley of the brook got more and more narrow and I soon found myself in a thicket of wild raspberry bushes growing high under the tall and sparse fir trees which looked like columns with feathery crowns. It was a lovely place where I had never been before. My horse, Shalunia stepped carefully, feeling the way as I could not guide it – the masses of raspberry bushes covered the ground like a thick, dark-green blanket. The bushes were tall and strong, grown in the semi-shade of the firs, and the masses of berries were astounding, the air was scented with their sweet smell. I could not stop eating, picking them with ease as their graceful shoots brushed my knees as I rode through the thicket. Even Shalunia seemed to be tempted by the smell and stopped to nibble some of the green (for I don't really think that she paid much attention to the berries). But suddenly she pricked up her ears and gave a snort accompanied by a restless shake of the head and the attentive playing of the ears. I looked around, for Shalunia behaved like this when she scented some big game close by. A little to my right, a few yards away, I noticed a spot where the raspberry bushes had been crushed, broken obviously by some large animal – and quite recently. As I bent down to pat Shalunia's neck to quiet her and said aloud something soothing – a sudden bounce and crashing of dry wood to my right made Shalunia jerk aside and I had just time to catch sight of a dark form diving into the thicket from the very bushes where I had been picking my best raspberries. It was a bear, who was obviously enjoying his berries as much as I was, and we had both had the

The engagement photograph of Edith to Count Alexander Sollohub in the summer of 1906. She was 20, he was 22. Edith was not looking forward to the responsibilities of marriage.

The salon in the St Petersburg apartment, furnished in the fashionable French style, with a grand piano for musical evenings.

A corner of the study in the St Petersburg apartment, Panteleimonskaya 12, where her father first helped Edith learn to read.

Kamenka, the country house of Count Alexander (Sasha) Sollohub, bought in 1903, used by Sasha and Edith as their family home until "nationalised" by the revolutionary authorities in December 1917. No photograph remains, but this sketch was later made from memory by one of their sons.

Count Alexander Sollohub standing beside two elk brought down "with a right and a left", i.e. using both barrels of the gun. The horse and groom in the photograph had been sent into the forest to bring the elk home. November 1906.

In the war years, Edith was often in charge of the Kamenka estate. In this 1916 photograph she was supervising the sale of timber stockpiled in the forest.

Alexander (centre of group) home on leave in 1917, discussing the serious political situation with friends. The friend on the right of the picture is Alphonse Riesenkampf.

Edith after a capercailzie shoot, with birds displayed on the gamekeeper's garden fence. c. 1917.

Waldensee, in Livonia, bought in the 1890s as a country residence conveniently placed for Professor Martens' travels to The Hague and other west European cities. On the right of the picture, his three young daughters are seated in a donkey-cart.

A traditional "lineika" used for travelling on rough tracks through the forest. 1917.

One of the boats used in the hunting expedition on Lake Ladoga with Alphonse Riesenkampf. 1918.

Showing a different style of hunting after the revolution, Edith went out alone with a gun in search of food. It amused her in 1918 to be, as it were, a poacher on nationalised land.

brilliant idea of picking them from the same bushes. The bear would have probably remained there without moving had not Shalunia snorted and had I not spoken aloud. When I looked at the crushed bushes closer, with Shalunia still very nervous and alert, I found that they were cleaned of their berries and were crushed by the bear who, having had his meal, had surely settled down there for a little siesta.

The other time I met a bear was in early spring, in April, when the snow still lay on the ground in the sheltered places and under the trees but had melted on the open spaces. I was out alone to stalk capercailzie during their night song. It is a most exciting and very difficult sport requiring a lot of attention. As I stood still under the trees, at dawn, listening for the desired song of the capercailzie, I suddenly heard heavy steps not far from me. Who could walk about in these forests at night – but a poacher! My heart beat fast – I listened – not a sound. That's it – the poacher is waiting too for the song and dares not move so as not to frighten the game – I thought. Minutes passed and then suddenly the song broke out. I listened for its flow and dashed forward in the direction of the bird, stopping short as the song broke off.

I thought I heard the poacher stopping too half a second after me. No doubt – he is doing what I do, stalking the same bird, and how shall I behave if we come face to face? My thoughts whirled: shall I let him go as if unnoticed? – No, that is cowardly, for we send our gamekeepers to stop poachers and here I, the owner, will let one slip undisturbed? This won't do. But if I stop him, what shall I do with him? He won't obey me if I order him to give up his gun – to me, to a woman! And if he doesn't – I should shoot – at least to frighten him, but he may shoot for good – an unpleasant prospect. These thoughts galloped through my mind, I stood motionless listening now again to the flowing ever more rapidly, the girgling song ending in the twitter of triumph, and then silence again. "Ah", I thought "he too, the poacher, has heard me and does not move to check my movements." I felt hot and cold clutching my gun – and there, in the perfect silence of the night, the heavy steps walking away, slouching steps, irregular and soft. "Strange," I thought as the sound died in the distance; it puzzled me why the man had gone – not a sportive poacher to make all that noise too where the capercailzie sing. When daylight came and there was no more possibility of stalking the capercailzie I retraced my steps to see on the snow where the poacher had gone to. And to my surprise and amusement I saw the footprints of a fair-sized bear. Probably he had scented me and stopped to listen for my steps, perhaps to locate where the danger was lurking. When he heard no noise he quietly went on his way, never bothering about me. It may have been luckier for me than I realised it at first, for in early spring they are hungry after the long winter fast and might attack men.

Sasha's Bear

We were sitting rather at a loose end on an early stormy and snowy February afternoon, unable to go out with the wind blowing, snowdrifts accumulating on the road, when the maid came in to say that Sidor would like to speak to Sasha. "Show him in" was Sasha's reply and we only wondered what Sidor could have to report on such a day. A moment later the man came in, his eyebrows and drooping moustache still wet from the snow he had evidently only just brushed off.

"Well, what's the hurry, Sidor? I did not expect you in this horrid weather," said Sasha.

"It is a blowy day for certain, Sir. I had only gone out this morning to see about some felling in the No. 22 district of Kudrovo and was stopped on my way back by one of the men working there who told me about bear tracks he had seen early this morning before the dirty weather set in."

"Bear tracks, where?" said Sasha, getting quite wide awake now.

"In the Kudrovskaia dacha, across the winter road that zig-zags along our border and the 'Kazennyi les'." I could not quite trust the man so I went there, through the front – not past the village – and found the spot. Bear tracks right enough, but difficult to make out what size for there was already plenty of snow covering them. I tried to peep at them a little further where they disappeared in the thicket and were not so snowed in yet. Looks like a good-sized bear, 9 to 10 Poods [approx. 160 kilos], I'd say. He went into our forest all right, but at this time of the year . . . one never knows . . . he must have been roused out of his winter sleep, perhaps by elk trampling near, perhaps by woodcutters . . . many wander before settling again.

"The road is on our land there?" put in Sasha.

"Yes, at this point, but he walked across the border very near there, may have been looping – I could not follow so as not to arouse suspicions among the kazenny keepers, you know, Sir . . ."

"You were right. If they notice the tracks they are sure to ask me for permission to take the bear in a shoot for Grand Duke M. . . . they are short of bears this year, I heard" said Sasha musingly.

"That's what I was afraid of, I know their gamekeeper is to pass this road tomorrow as he is expected at Kudrovo, he is sure to notice – even with this snow – the tracks are deep enough!" added Sidor with a sigh.

"I suppose then there is nothing we can do," said Sasha reluctantly, "unless you have some suggestion, Sidor?"

In fact I was waiting for this question as I knew that Sidor would not give up a good case without trying to win it somehow, and Sasha knew it too.

"You see, Sir, there would be a possibility . . . one could brush over the tracks . . . on the winter road . . . the kazenny gamekeepers would not notice anything . . ." and Sidor stopped.

"But what?" asked Sasha, raising his eyebrows.

"Sir, if I passed in a sledge through the village of Kudrovo to reach the winter road . . . to brush . . . everyone there would wonder why I went in a sledge and not on foot . . . word spreads quickly . . . it might be a nuisance in the end."

"I see you are right," said Sasha musingly. "In fact, I have to go to those parts to see about the felling district assigned to Kudrovo men . . . I could perhaps see to something?"

Sidor's face beamed. "This is just what I had been thinking, Sir. And if the Countess went too . . . it might be better still – a drive. Also it might be easier about the brushing . . . Only it is pretty rough outside still, Kudrovo might wonder . . ."

"Don't worry, I'll see to that. At what distance from Kudrovo could the tracks be?"

"At about two and a half to three miles, Sir, in the fir tree thicket, the first after a small clearing with a stack of old wood nearby," Sidor hurried to say. "May I order the sledge, Sir?"

"Yes, order the heavier sledge with old Seraia," said Sasha, adding with a smile, "She is such a lumpy horse that she will kick up all the snow she can if I try to move her off the road." Sidor laughed understandingly and disappeared in a hurry with a "Yes Sir".

"Now we are off on a poacher's trick," said Sasha with a pleased chuckle. "Dress warmly and be ready quickly, there is no time to be lost as we should be through Kudrovo village as early as possible in the afternoon. See to our skis being put in the sledge, please."

Ten minutes later we were driving towards Kudrovo with the skis sticking out between us and old Seraia treading heavily in the soft fresh snow. A five-mile drive can seem very slow in a snowstorm, but fortunately the wind subsided when we entered the forest and we covered the distance quicker than we had hoped to. As we drove through Kudrovo Sasha asked a man who was just unloading wood near his izba whether he had been working in the district we were going to. The man said no as it was his brother's district who had started work there last week. Thanking him for the information, Sasha mentioned casually that once out he might go there and have a look. So on we went across the opening on which Kudrovo lay and penetrated into the dense forest beyond, following the small winding winter road, in fact only a track trodden down by the villagers going out on lumber work. These winding roads allowed for the narrow track left by a peasant's sledge and looked rather like a ditch in the soft cushion-like snow banks on either side. The heavily laden branches of the fir trees hung low over our heads, shedding at times their load of snow on our heads.

"No one seems to have been driving here recently, not today anyhow," said Sasha, "look at the thick snow on the branches."

"The better," I answered, enjoying the perfect peace and great silence of the place. The snow was still falling but in a more regular, quiet way, not in drifts blown by the wind.

"Look out now," said Sasha suddenly. "Keep an eye on your side of the road, I'll watch over the other and turn into the bank as if making way for a coming sledge". He slowed Seraia's pace, who was trotting heavily and slowly anyhow.

"There it is!" called out Sasha a moment later, "On my side, that's it. Too late to brush it out, leave it for the return. Mind your side now. Stand up and look well in advance. The bear will probably have walked a few paces along the trodden-down road."

I was up peering anxiously in front of me. There was some uneven snow on my side. "Stop," I called out, "on my left, about six yards ahead!"

Sasha pulled at the reins, guiding Seraia into the snow bank on my side, calling out at the same time, "Put your left leg well out, let it sweep on the snow as far out as you can!" I obeyed the order and, grabbing the side of the sledge, let myself be dragged across the tracks over which we were just passing just before they vanished in the thicket.

"They were the bear's tracks all right," said Sasha with satisfaction when the sledge bumped back with a thud into the road. "Did you try to stamp your feet?" he asked with some concern.

"I did, as much as I could, as if I were trying to get the sledge into balance again," I said.

"That's all right. Now we have to drive on for a couple of miles and we'll see what can be done then. Keep a good look out anyhow." We drove on in silence. I did not know exactly on whose land the tracks we had brushed out were, and wondered whether Sasha knew, but I preferred not to ask him. Presently, having driven another two or three miles, we got out of the sledge, put on our skis and walked along a clearing into the forest. We soon reached the district where some work had begun before the snowstorm, Sasha went round looking at various marks on trees, then we returned to where we had left Seraia and drove back slowly along the same road we had come.

"Hold on now!" called out Sasha all of a sudden, "I'll turn out of the rut as we did before, as if meeting another sledge again. Better do it once or twice before we get to the proper spot." Up went the sledge on his side, Seraia ploughing unwillingly into the deep snow, probably wondering why as there was no obvious reason, and I holding on to the side tightly as we bumped back into the track. "All right! We'll get practice. The first tracks must be near here, there's the stack of dry wood. Yes, here it is. Hold tight!"

I certainly did hold tight and noticed how Sasha jumped out of the sledge, stamping the snow sideways and holding on to the reins, forcing Seraia to back and pull on again. It certainly looked as if someone had had a lot of trouble with his sledge. Sasha did a similar manoeuvre so well over one or two more places that I really could not remember which was the "dangerous spot".

"Now," sighed Sasha, "I think this is done and we can go back hoping for the best." He smiled contentedly under his snow-covered moustache and I dug my face deeper into my fur collar. The snow was falling steadily, silently, not driven by the wind anymore.

All the following days we waited anxiously for news of fresh traces, for rumours or for requests from the Imperial Hunt headquarters. We feared the local "bush telegraph", which seemed to function in our wild snow-covered North quite as efficiently as in the depths of Africa. Sidor obviously guessed what we had done but by tacit agreement the episode was not mentioned. He kept a very close watch on all tracks in his Kudrovskaia dacha but had nothing new to report. It really was a relief when a fortnight later, counting on the bear having settled – even though precariously – for a second winter's rest, Sasha decided to try our luck. And it really meant trying our luck since the bear would probably be on the alert and would have to be driven on to one gun only. As I had never yet seen a bear in a drive Sasha would not let me stand alone even though Sidor had suggested he could stand with me and a spare gun.

So off we went with beaters, red rags and all gamekeepers in sledges and with skis. The district where the bear was supposed to be was duly surrounded with flags, we were put on the narrow space left unprotected, and the beat began. The day was clear, the frost not too sharp and there was no wind. The shouts of the beaters approached quickly. I listened and looked, scarcely daring to breathe as I stood a step behind Sasha, gun in hand and with the order not to shoot unless it was necessary (for me to judge, I

supposed). Suddenly excited shouts of: "Take care, Andrei, here
. . . Andrei . . ." I could not understand what it all meant but
noticed that Sasha drew up his shoulders, leaning slightly
forward. Then he suddenly lifted his gun and the shot went.
I could not see a thing behind his back and only murmured:
"You've got it surely!" and thought that, after all, I had not seen
the bear in the forest, as I was meant to before being allowed
to have a stand.

"I've got him all right," called out Sasha as Sidor came running
along the track. "But what were these shouts about Andrei in the
beat?" Sasha was asking now as we walked up to the black mass I
could see now near a bunch of small fir trees.

"I don't know, Sir, but here is Andrei," Sidor replied, and he
pointed out towards a young beater who was ploughing his way
through the deep snow. Andrei was beaming.

"Did the bear try to eat you, Andrei?" asked Sasha half-
jokingly.

"Not quite so, Sir," answered Andrei, laughing, "but he grinned
and wanted to hug me, I think!"

"No wonder he wanted to if you smiled at him as you do now
. . . But seriously, what did happen?" asked Sasha.

"I was pushing my way through a thicket and had stopped
shouting," said Andrei with his broad smile, "when suddenly the
bear popped out from the thicket and stopped and showed me
his ugly grin. I yelled something and beat the bush hard with my
stick – and the bear was gone with a growl. Probably my yell
frightened him."

"No wonder, it frightened me all right," I put in. "It is a good
lesson and I'll know what to do if I ever meet a bear in the
forest."

We looked at the animal as it lay there in the snow, a mass
of very dark brown thick fur. We were all delighted that Sasha
got him, for our brushing manoeuvres had been weighing on
our minds and we'd been dreading either a request from the
Imperial Hunt or complicated explanations. But fortunately our
first and only poacher's manoeuvre had been carried out as a
clean job.

My First Bear

It was the first time that I stood alone on the stand for a bear shoot. Until then I had accompanied my husband and had been allowed to shoot after his first shot, if the bear needed a second one. This had actually happened once and experts had judged then that my bullet had been placed as well as that of my husband's first shot. Consequently he graciously allowed me to share with him in the honour of having taken this bear. It thus figured in my list as "half a bear on December 14, 1908". However, I was now considered a fully fledged bear hunter and was put on my own stand, the second in a line of four. Sidor stood behind me with a spare gun, for "my use", my husband told me, but I suspect that Sidor had orders to use it himself if necessary.

And so, there I was waiting for my opportunity, on a mild March morning with mountains of snow, light frost, grey mist drifting slowly through the forest. The beat starts – a strange disturbance in these perfectly silent surroundings where I scarcely dare move. I listen to the growing rumour but all my attention is in my eyes. Then suddenly, fifty yards in front of me, the large and bulky figure of a bear appears, coming towards me in clumsy bounds, heavy and swift at the same time, somewhat rolling in his gait. His head is slightly raised, his little bead-like eyes set closely together lock restlessly from side to side, I can follow their movement.

Sidor pushes my arm slightly; my gun is ready, finger on the trigger. I only wait for the right moment to raise it to my shoulder. Now – the bear is near, he turns slightly sideways – and with a quick movement I raise the gun and press the trigger. A bang, I sway back from the shock, and look in vain for the bear somewhere to the left.

"He's down! Grand! Marvellous!" calls out Sidor, and his voice strikes me as being terribly loud, as loud as the shot, after the silence of the expectation and the occasional whispers exchanged ever since we were near the beat.

"Where is he?" I ask, bewildered, still looking left in the direction the bear was going.

"There, straight in front of us," says Sidor, pointing to a black form half hidden by small fir trees.

Yes, there he is, my first bear, lying cuddled, his nose dug into the snow, poor beast! I hate looking at him now and feel disgusted with myself. Such a beauty, so dark and so large too, and only a few minutes ago he had been turning his little eyes so swiftly right and left. Why had I shot him?

"Well done, congratulations, a beauty . . . and one straight shot too!" voices say all round me, and my husband puts his hand on my shoulder in appreciation.

Sidor goes back on the track, shows where the bear came out and how he had come and where he had turned showing me his flank. My gun felt suddenly so heavy on my arm and I leaned it against a tree.

"Come and see your excellent hit," said my husband.

Sidor, bending down, raised the bear's head holding it by the ears. And there, all of a sudden, the little eyes turned again right and left, it must be an illusion, I must be dreaming.

"Let go, Sidor!" calls my husband sharply, pulling a Browning out of his pocket.

A short dry pistol shot in the ear puts a definite end to my first bear. I was horrified to have seen those small eyes again; this last semiconscious movement of the eyes had marred the pleasure I felt at having made a fine, clear shot.

The next day we, the bear and I, were photographed together in front of the house. Strangely enough this photograph was later picked out by the correspondent of the *London Illustrated News* who had come to Russia in search of typical pictures of this country. In a special number devoted to Russia three or four photographs of winter shooting taken in our Kamenka estate were published, and among them mine with my first bear. As I look now at this photograph, one of the few that I still have from home, I see in the sad expression with which I look down at the bear a reflection of the feelings that haunted me at the time – so many years ago – feelings of regret, doubt and nearly shame, but I do remember that I was quite proud too.

Unexpected Luck

It was the last day of October 1912. The first snowstorm of the season was raging. The wind was bitterly cold and drove the snow into narrow ridges along the hedges of the high road and the drive. We were expecting our usual set of friends who came more or less every weekend for our shoots.

"Late as usual," muttered my husband, passing through the dining room where a bright blaze in the huge open fireplace looked inviting and cheerful. He hated the meals to be late and it was already half past seven, our dinner time. Upstairs the noise in the nurseries had quieted down: both little boys had been safely tucked in and had their goodnight kiss from me. I sat in blissful laziness in a deep armchair and mused on tomorrow's shooting prospects after this raging storm.

Suddenly the Samoyed curled at my feet jumped up with a loud bark. The snorting of horses was heard under the windows – there they were, one, two, three sledges.

"Indeed, I never thought it was so trying to be a sportsman in winter," came out of the dark the voice of a friend who, in fact, was coming out for his first shoot, never having tried this sport before. Into the bright light of the lantern at the door emerged the stiff figure of a tall, lean man, donned in a splendid fur coat with fur cap, fur gloves, fur muff and white felt boots, valenki, reaching far above the knees.

"What makes you regret already your first attempts at shooting in winter? And that before you had even had time to take your gun out of its presumably fur-lined case?" laughed my husband.

"You would not laugh if you had had to fight during the thirty miles ride against Baron B's dog who sat on our lap and insisted on licking my face," was the reply.

"Harras, Harras . . . down, Harras!" shouted in vain the owner of the too-friendly dog trying to stop his favourite from sniffing at the hors d'oeuvres prepared on a side table in the dining room.

"What made you so late anyhow?" grumbled my husband. "Didn't you catch the three-thirty train?" But throwing a glance at two of the other guests laboriously getting out of their numerous wraps, he only gave a low whistle, very expressive if not exactly very well bred.

I knew what this meant and had immediately an extra bottle of vodka taken away from the table. The cold, the long sleigh drive, the fact alone of getting out of the everyday routine were

good reasons enough for arranging a kind of picnic on the road;
it had become quite a custom by now with our numerous friends.
The result was that they never felt hungry on arriving, but were
abnormally thirsty – and visibly tired. Wasting no time over dinner
they generally were glad to rest in the deep armchairs near the fire
or on the huge old-fashioned red plush sofa in the small salon.
One or two of the hardier ones withstood this temptation of a rest
and either played billiards with us or played the piano, to my great
delight. By half past ten, when the evening tea with sandwiches
was served, they would all regain their lively spirits and start a game
of poker which lasted well into the night, champagne keeping up
their strength. Servants were sent to bed. The champagne was
naturally "frappé" as we put it into the mounds of snow swept
up at the steps of the terrace. More than once, when the snow
melted down in spring, we discovered forgotten bottles in these
disappearing mounds and drank them to the health of our winter
guests!

"Breakfast at eight and we start at nine" had been the order
given by my husband, and sleepy faces were down at eight in the
grey light of a dull November morning.

Sidor, with his yellow drooping moustache and small blue eyes,
stood in the hall ready to take any orders or to help the guests in
their preparations.

"I have two odd 12-bore ball cartridges – do you want them?"
said one of the hoarse voices to me.

"Thank you. They might come in useful. Slip them into my
coat pocket, it's in the hall."

The eight gamekeepers were lined up in front of the house, the
beaters were waiting on the road – one could hear them joking
and laughing. Upstairs two little cheerful faces were looking out
of the nursery windows. From somewhere came the distressed
bark of my Samoyed, locked up for fear that he would follow me.
Harras, feeling superior, was proudly endeavouring to wag the
short stump of a tail left him by fashion.

The day was grey, the wind had quieted down, the snow
covered but lightly the hard frozen ground. The first beat was
near the house – with the usual hares, two or three scared rabbits
rushing for their burrows. From the very beginning we seemed

to have good luck: the air was quiet and clear, the beaters had an easy task as the ground was frozen, the snow had scarcely penetrated into the thick of the forest; the game rose easily and in good numbers. After the first three or four beats all guns had had excellent chances and the bag promised to be better than we had expected. Hares, the grey so-called field hares, were particularly numerous, hazel hens had been easy to raise and three heather cocks had been brought down. As to the white forest hares, they were giving us a lot of fun. I say "us" thinking more of the others than of myself, for I seemed to have a decidedly bad day as no game had come my way all through the morning. I could barely boast of a couple of hares and one hazel hen.

"Did you by chance meet an old woman this morning on starting?" one of our friends asked me, alluding to a current superstition according to which old women bring ill luck to the sportsman.

"Well, I did see nurse – and she was cross besides – but I am pretty sure that I saw my maid first, and she is young enough, and well drilled never to wish us good speed when we go out shooting," I said, remembering another favourite superstition.

At lunch, which was served some four miles from home, the topic of my bad luck came up again. Baron B insisted on changing places with me at the next stand and to keep then to this new order. As I refused he said, "Don't you see how tired my poor Harras is? He has been dragging my hares and birds out of the thicket all the morning and—"

"And making a jolly nuisance of himself," put in my husband.

"In fact I only heard 'Harras, here, Harras . . . there' and all my hares scampered away before I could shoot them, as Harras snorted like an engine in the thicket."

"Harras is a bit deaf – you must excuse his old age. But let us change places with your wife and I won't be your neighbour anymore – and you'll get all your hares in peace."

"No, thank you, I trust in fate," I said, "and besides, I prefer not to be too near the critical eye of my husband – he so easily finds fault with my shooting."

Thus we left things as fate had decided and resumed our sport after a short and light lunch.

It grew colder, heavy grey clouds hung low, there was snow in the air. My fingertips began to feel the cold – and my luck was as far away from me as ever. I did not mind it, however, as I always enjoyed being out in the forests and cared little for the shoots with beaters. There was no real sport in them – they looked to me like a kind of butchery on a more or less extensive scale.

By four o'clock both sportsmen and beaters were somewhat tired, the light was fading and we were on the point of turning home when my husband gave the order to take another beat, a short one. I took my stand, the first on the right wing this time, and close against the thick brushwood with the ride behind me. A similar wall of small thick undergrowth rose on the other side of the ride. I was downright cold by now, and hanging my gun over my arm, slipped both hands deep into the side pockets of my short jacket. I contemplated sadly the few empty spaces in my cartridge belt. Nothing much could be expected from this last beat – perhaps a few forest hares, some heather cocks at best.

The horn rang out soon, blurred in the misty evening air, the beaters' shouts rose still lustily. I stood a little unconcerned and inattentive when the sound of heavy treads right in front of me attracted my attention. Who could walk about there? I knew there was no felling in these parts; it might be elk, I thought, and realised that both barrels were loaded with shot. Yes, but the ball cartridges of X? He wanted to slip them into my pocket this morning. I fumbled right and left – here was one. In a second the gun was ready: ball in the right, small shot in the choke. The footsteps were approaching – stopping – going on nearer – quite near now. I scanned the bushes, but the brushwood of young fir was impenetrable. A black shadow to my left – but how low for an elk? The gun ready in my arm – my eyes followed the black form – here it is near the ride – a step away from it – and a bear leapt heavily across the ride, some thirty yards away – not to shoot along the stands, the thought flashes across my mind and my finger presses the trigger – I can't see anything but I hear the angry growl in the bushes across the ride – then another low growl.

The beaters are near – but the boundary of the Imperial shooting grounds is also near, and the bear is wounded once he growls so near the spot where I shot – he can make straight for this Imperial shoot – and what a fuss then to get the permission to follow the track . . . All these thoughts flashed through my mind like lightning, I saw the displeased expression on my husband's face, I heard him say drily: "If you can't shoot a bear on the spot, don't do it at all . . ." and off I was through the thicket after the bear. A bright spot of clear blood on the scanty snow at the edge of the brushwood where I had shot – a lung wound, I thought – and I followed the track swiftly. Pretty badly hurt, the bear growled and grunted close to me – I followed the sounds endeavouring to reload my gun with the remaining ball cartridge – but where was it? – Yes, here I found it in another pocket – the gun is ready – the growls are near now, the tread is heavy, slow, uneven. But this desperate brushwood – our pride of young fir trees – how I cursed them now. It was quite dark there, I could make my way with difficulty, stumbling against roots, moss-covered rotten trunks – and the growls were growing more and more distinct, right in front of me – and I still couldn't see a thing. Facing a bear at arm's length in these bushes seems a stupid thing to do – and to let him escape is a shame. If only I could see him! Lying down flat on the moss I at last caught sight of a black form – apparently the bear sitting on his haunches, groaning – some ten yards from me. I level my gun and shoot – a fierce growl, branches break, a heavy bounce. At the same moment my husband's hand grabs me by the collar and drags me by force out of the thicket.

"What? Running after a wounded bear? How unsportsmanlike," he was saying.

I felt dreadfully small and wrong.

The gamekeepers were rushing up towards us – the rumour of the bear had spread as my neighbour had sighted it crossing the ride. Having no ball cartridges he did not dare follow me but had shouted the news along the line of guns to my husband who was one of the last. Already Sidor was taking a shortcut through the forest to the right, others came from the left – we waited a few minutes – hours to me – then the horn rang out – the bear was found. We rushed into the thicket again – and some ten yards from the spot where I had fired my second bullet, we found the dead bear surrounded by the men. A fine dark bear weighing 24 stone, as we saw later. A bullet through both lungs, entering right above the left shoulder – and no other bullet. Congratulations – a good pat on the shoulder from my husband, a warm embrace from the oldest gamekeeper – an old and dear friend of mine – exclamations of joy, surprise, of wonder.

And I? Didn't I feel small and still smaller? And wasn't it a pity to have killed this lovely beast? But it would perhaps have gone into the forests of the Imperial shoot – some Grand Duke would have taken it there – and I grudged them my bear in good old neighbourly rivalry and competition. Besides, my husband was pleased now – even proud of me.

Well, it was a nice evening and when the bear was hauled into the hall later on my little boys came to look at it, scarcely daring to approach it, the bigger one trying to look unconcerned like a man, but shuddering slightly when his father smeared with the bear's blood a sign on the boy's forehead – for the boy to grow into a brave huntsman, says the superstition.

My Last Bear

Spring on the calendar, 10 April 1915, but severe winter weather outside; masses of snow after days of gales, snowfalls and snowdrifts. An exhausting winter too, with war news none too good, and nerve strain growing with daily increasing difficulties in the economic conditions of life. Worst of all, perhaps, the growing inner dissatisfaction throughout the country and the semi-conscious apprehension of some approaching disaster. It seemed that the dark winter could not leave us, that spring could not break the spell and cheer us.

The depressing atmosphere of town – Petrograd – had been too much for me and I was glad that I had to leave it again in order to see to the management of our country estate. My husband being in the army, the agent and several of the foresters having been called up, it had been my task since the very outbreak of war to manage the much-loved forest estate, and the task – although an arduous one – had given me much joy and helped me over the worries and anxieties for those at the front. It had given me plenty of opportunities, too, to hunt and track game, to learn to love and understand our northern nature. The forests were without end, one great mass of land with large stretches of bogs and moors, with narrow bands of meadows along rivers and brooks with small villages – lonely on their open glades turned into fields.

I had tracked lynx and elk, made attempts at tracking wolves, which were scarce in these parts, and spent hours skiing after deer and hares. But I had never had the opportunity of tracking a bear – perhaps I would not have ventured to do it, as a bear is rare, a "kingly game" in these parts, and I never had too much self-confidence or faith in my skill. What would my husband have said if I had tracked a bear the wrong way, tracked him over our boundary, to be shot by someone in the Imperial Hunt? I do not think I would ever have been forgiven, and this mistake would certainly have weighed heavily on me – heavily as such mistakes can weigh only on someone who is still pretty young.

These thoughts of bears were occupying me that evening as I drove home from a concert through the brightly lit streets of Petrograd, noiseless with the deep carpet of snow and swiftly passing sledges. In fact, three days previously, before the last snowfall, a large bear had been sighted approaching our boundary, even making a loop into our grounds but finally walking out of them. This was the report our oldest gamekeeper, Ivan Ivanovich, had given me just as I was leaving the country to bring my children to town for the coming Easter Holidays.

I could not delay the departure, as all preparations had been made – nurses, governesses, little boys were all dressed in their fur coats waiting excitedly to get into the sledges. Much to my disappointment I had to carry on my part of good mother and head of the family and push down my evident desire to stay on and to follow tomorrow the movements of the bear, on which Ivan Ivanovich would keep an eye. Bad luck, I thought, more than once during these last three days, especially as the newly fallen snow was sure to have blurred and destroyed all possible tracks.

Good news, however, awaited me at home. Sidor had come from the country an hour before to say that the bear had been tracked on one of the good beats. The animal was apparently restless, having been roused too soon out of his winter sleep, and was wandering about the country. No time could be lost and we had to "take him" tomorrow if at all.

According to Ivan Ivanovich, who had tracked the bear, the animal must be a very large one, though not fat. This last statement amused me, and Sidor explained that the footprints were those of a large bear in size, but their imprint on the fresh snow did not reach as deep as they should have done, and the animal seemed to "skim" the surface. The more reason to hurry, as the bear might not be interested in staying long on the beat, although the place should suit him – according to Sidor's idea of a bear's taste.

The beat was large with dense thicket all along the line where the animal would be sure to go. This meant that one gun, myself alone, would not be sufficient to guard the line.

My thoughts immediately turned to two men who were keen sportsmen, and had asked me more than once to let them try their luck at a bear hunt. An hour later everything had been fixed and Sidor left by the last night train. Ivan Ivanovich was to check up at dawn on the whereabouts of the bear and to see about our arrival at noon. We were to be two stands but three guns. One was the Japanese Ambassador, who had known me since my childhood, and whom I had to invite at once. The other gun was an old friend, a Polish member of the State Council, Mr D, a good shot and an experienced huntsman who had asked to come as a second gun on my stand, being keener on the sight than on a shot.

Thus, by noon the next day we were all on the spot, a bit stiff after the very long drive, huddled in furs and unable to move in the felt-lined sledges with heavy fur rugs. On the way we had picked up another "second gun" to stand with the Japanese Ambassador. It was our dear old friend and neighbour, Mr K, the head forester of the Imperial Hunt, a keen lover of forests and a poor shot. I suspected that he wanted to come in order to try out on the Japanese his knowledge of French, and English, which he had learnt all by himself without ever having heard a Frenchman or an Englishman speak their language and which he, therefore, conscientiously pronounced on the basis of the Latin alphabet. His English was especially original and had given me a moment of consternation when he had first tried it on me with a poem by Byron.

The long fur coats had to be abandoned in the sledges, as we had to ski to the stands. Mr K struggled into a kind of large nightshirt pulled over his brown shooting coat, making remarks in supposedly French or English about his unwieldy figure and his difficulty in moving on skis. The Japanese Ambassador, very small and very round, especially when hidden in his thick furs, was eyeing with terror the pair of skis which a gamekeeper was trying to fix to his felt boots. The beaters crowding round us were gaping open-mouthed at the strange figure, and they even forgot their usual jokes and giggles, as they whispered remarks to one another, puzzled about the unusual-looking visitor.

Finally, two sturdy old beaters had to take the Ambassador under their elbows and, wading themselves through the deep snow, they half supported, half carried him up to the stand where he was safely deposited behind small firs with the old Mr K towering behind him. They had drawn No. 1 stand – much to the distress of Ivan Ivanovich who came up to me, his cap pushed over his eyebrows, scratching vigorously behind his right ear – a sure sign of worry with him.

"Too bad they have stand No. 1: that bear is sure to go that way, I am positive . . . well, something will have to be done," he muttered. I pretended I had not heard the last words, for I guessed what that something would be and could not very well sanction it – being the hostess.

Noiselessly we approached stand No. 2; the men continued their way. The flags were there already – I could see them in the distance where Ivan had placed them in the early morning. We had to wait now for the flankers to take up position, as beaters should not be posted in advance since the least noise would rouse the bear and the strong smell of the beaters' sheepskin coats might make him suspicious.

The edge of the thicket was to my left; sparse firs, young aspen, tall birches and groups of mixed underwood stretched out in front of us. It had been decided that I would shoot first and Mr D would be ready to step in should I miss. The first blank shots – and the drive began, so distant, muffled in the snow-laden atmosphere, so familiar yet always exciting. As the noise came nearer, I realised that it was much louder and clearer on the left and barely distinguishable on the right. Something must have gone wrong and I suddenly remembered the "something" of Ivan Ivanovich and could not refrain from smiling as I visualised him now leading his right flank, his wrinkled face wearing a worried expression, whistling low signals to keep his men back, hissing to the nearest his orders not to shout. The result of his tactics was soon apparent – first a slight crackling of branches, the dull sound of falling clumps of snow from bent bushes, then right in front of us the glimpse of a dark figure among the bushes.

The bear with his rolling trot, broken by jerks and bounds as he made his way between rotten trunks of trees and clumps of willow bushes, could now be clearly seen. He was making straight for us; my gun lay ready on my arm. It was a large bear, for in spite of the deep snow he was looming well above the surface, a compact dark mass, the neck stretched out, the black nose slightly turned up, the ears two black tufts on the somewhat lighter head. He looked preoccupied, very busy in choosing the right way. Once or twice he cast a quick glance over his right shoulder – evidently the shots and the shouts coming from that direction annoyed him. Mr D touched me gently on the shoulder – should I shoot? No, never shoot *de face* – that was my husband's invariable injunction, and experience had shown me that in the case of big game the rule was good.

Still, I began to doubt as the bear came nearer, and I could see even his small restless eyes. He came closer still; was it ten, perhaps eight yards? I lifted my gun and fired, aiming at the root of the neck. The kick of my husband's heavy double-barrelled rifle sent me stumbling backwards as I suddenly saw the huge figure of the bear swinging forward to fall at our feet with a growl. Another shot, Mr D's – and all was quiet. Guns in hand we stood ready to shoot again, but the big heavy body only twitched, the head dug deep into the snow. How glad I was I had not seen his eyes – those little yellow eyes which looked so fiercely at me a second ago somewhere high above me. "You waited a little too long," said Mr D, smiling, "it might have been rather unpleasant."

Upon closer examination of the bear it was found that my

bullet had cut the arteries of the throat, and the bullet of Mr D's lighter rifle had broken the forearm of the right paw as the bear stood on his haunches. Apparently mortally wounded, the animal had made one last attempt to hurl himself against the enemy and had collapsed in the effort. He was a magnificent beast weighing 480 lbs.

Among the beaters was our foreman, the Tartar Ismail, whose hobby was photography. He carried his large camera with him wherever he could and he now fetched it from the sledges. We laughed at the time at his zeal and energy, but today I am glad he succeeded in taking this photograph, which turned out to be the last taken of a bear hunt at home, and one of the very few remaining in my possession.

How happy Ivan Ivanovich was at the outcome of the hunt! He had pressed my shoulder and in his quick whisper, with so many colourful local expressions, had told me as we walked back to the sledges, "It is good that you took the bear. I could not think of that little yellow gentleman having him. My dreams and my fortune had warned me that there would be great difficulties, but had also told me that the bear would come out where I wanted him to. The men could not understand why I delayed and kept them back – it was a difficult beat – the bear wanted to go left. He is a beauty – the best you have ever got and a clean shot."

I was glad and happy in Ivan Ivanovich's praise, and little did I think that this would be my last bear and my last bear hunt at home.

6

SMALL GAME AND OTHER STORIES FROM KAMENKA

Capercailzie

Somehow I find it very difficult to put down on paper my impressions of the capercailzie singing in spring and the passage of the wild swan in autumn. Perhaps I took these impressions too keenly – I was very young, and they became part of me. It is hard to write about something that is part of one's inner self.

Throughout the years that separate me from these experiences and in spite of the complete change of climate, surroundings and conditions of life I still find myself listening today to the wind rising on an early spring night and thinking, "Too bad, it will be hard to approach the capercailzie tonight." And when the quiet drizzle of a spring rain drips from the eaves in the quiet of the evening – I can see once more the big log fire at home, I feel the plush of the old armchair in which I sit and doze waiting for Sidor to tap on the window calling, "It is time to go, my Lady!"

In April 1919 there was no Sidor and I sat alone in my town house – not taken from us yet, whereas all estates and all money had been taken over a year ago.

Still, I was young, I loved the country and our forests, I knew the capercailzie was singing his spring song by now – I just *had* to try my luck once again. A kind friend, who had often been at our shoots and who had adequate documents – for the moment! – allowing him to move around more or less undisturbed, volunteered to go with me. We set out one morning with rucksacks and cartridge bags, in heavy marsh boots and warm clothes. After the short railway trip of an hour and a half we started on our expedition to my old home Kamenka. I had never done this journey on foot, of course – a good 23 miles – but this did not frighten me and I knew that at the end of 12 miles of straight road through absolutely uninhabited forest country we were sure to find shelter for the night at the friendly house of old D. Kravchinsky, Head Forestry Manager of the District. He lived in the only village we were to go through on our way to Kamenka. There too was the local Soviet or National Committee, as it was then called, and I counted upon them to let me have for these two or three days my guns, which had been taken from my house. There was in fact a sort of "gentlemen's agreement" between the Committee and myself by virtue of which they would let me use my guns if I undertook to bring them back. And I must say they stuck to this agreement – quite the gentlemen! The only snag was that I could not very well tell them where I was planning to shoot as my estate was nationalised and there might have been some objections to allowing me – the former owner – to shoot there. Still, this did not worry me, I was an incurable optimist.

We set out, walked, leisurely, lunched on sandwiches on a heap of stones as the ground was still covered with snow or with icy water. The friendly household of Kravchinsky received us with open arms – fed us, gave us beds, and Mr Kravchinsky arranged for us to go shooting that very night in the forests still under his control – more or less! The Committee proved once more to be quite gentlemanly and let me have two of my guns, one for each of us, and my small rifle, which I used in spring for black cocks on marshy meadows.

This first night of shooting was not what I really liked, because, not being acquainted with these parts, I had to go with one of the local foresters. For me the whole charm of shooting is being alone to work it out by myself. I had no luck, perhaps my heart was not in it; but my companion got his capercailzie all right.

After a short rest we continued our way, reaching my own gamekeepers lodge in a forest glade in the late afternoon. It lay near two of our best "toka" where I planned to go the next night.

Perhaps I had better explain what "tok", or "toka" in plural, means, and how the capercailzie is tackled. I'll try to be short and clear.

Every spring the male capercailzie choose a particular spot in the wildest part of the forest, where for a time they meet daily, or rather nightly, to sing their love song before dawn. This meeting place is called "tok". It is not easy to ascertain where a good tok is, unless a watch is kept on the movement of the birds well beforehand, for towards the end of winter, in February, the cocks assemble during daylight on the snow and "dance" with lowered wings like turkeys, preening themselves and puffing. The tracks on the snow show the points selected, although the cocks try out various spots before making up their mind. Usually they return year after year to the same old places unless some human activity in the neighbourhood makes them abandon them. The gamekeepers' duty was to keep a watch on these toka to make sure the birds have come in at the very start of the season, to check their approximate numbers and, of course, to keep an eye on poachers.

When the courting time starts the male birds come to the tok soon after sunset and start a series of throat-clearing exercises, gurgling, choking and producing strange noises which made me think, when I first heard them, that they were all desperately seasick. They all perch on the old pine and fir trees not too close to each other and remain there for the night. With the setting in of darkness, complete silence reigns on the tok, and it always thrilled me to creep away as noiselessly as possible knowing that the place was alive with big birds above me.

We generally stayed near a campfire, a mile or so away, waiting for dawn before returning to the tok. In the best song season, which is the middle of April, the first faint signs of approaching dawn show between one-thirty and two o'clock. Soon after the first call of the cranes on the marshes and sometimes before the first flight of duck the capercailzie begins to gurgle, first tentatively but soon breaking out into the proper song. In fact, it is not a song at all but an abrupt noise rather like gurgling at short intervals, these intervals becoming shorter and shorter until they sound like liquid being poured out of a bottle – the finish, a totally different sound, is something like the twitter of a number of small birds. At the moment when the twitter starts the ears of the capercailzie close inside so that he becomes completely deaf. His name in Russian and in Polish implies this – "glukhar" in Russian and "gluszec" in Polish, both based on "glukhoi", meaning deaf. The song lasts only a few minutes and the twitter is only a matter of a few seconds.

One must reach the tok before the birds awake and wait in the dark. They are extremely shy birds and as any movement or noise can frighten them into silence for quite a long time or set them into flight it is safer to wait until several cocks start singing and then decide upon the nearest to approach. A step can only be taken during the twitter, when the bird is deaf, and probably also blinded by passion, as movement at this particular moment does not seem to disturb it much. At the appropriate moment you dash forward in the direction you think your bird must be – a dash of four strides at most – and then stop dead just before the end of the twitter. Whether you finish your dash on both feet or on one, on your knees or on your stomach, you dare not move, and as the forests chosen for the tok are the wildest and it is still pitch dark under the trees there is every chance of having to stop in a most inconvenient position and to remain so until the next song! Even when within range of the tree or group of trees where you expect the bird to be, you cannot be sure of your shot – for the bird is not easy to see in the dark branches of the pine trees. More than once it happened that I "saw" him, a dark blob against the faint light of the sky, I shot "under the song", or in other words during the twitter, and found a thick cluster of branches falling – and strangely enough the bird not flying away as long as no shot had passed too closely to it, proving the extent of its deafness during the twitter. This is a long description of the technique of the approach alone, but each single case is different and I defy anyone to say it is an easy sport as you shoot the sitting bird. To get to it within shooting range is the art and to work your way up to the bird in a clean manner without disturbing others, quickly enough too to give yourself the chance of approaching another before the full daylight disperses them – this is an art that needs practice.

Well, this is what I loved doing, what I learnt by spending night after night in the forests, on the edges of bogs, listening to the voices of the forest and enjoying every minute. I did it for the last time those three nights spent in my "nationalised" estate.

I went alone that first night "at home". Ivan Pavlov, the gamekeeper, took me to within 100 to 150 yards of the tok and left me there to do the work alone at daybreak, for he had to take my friend to the other tok about a couple of miles away. All went well – no noises, dawn came, the first flight of duck passed and the first cocks started – I forgot revolution and communists and only felt the life of the forest around me. The tok was in full swing. I counted some 25 cocks and took my first one pretty quickly, neatly from the edge of the assembly, and had time to take one more – less successfully as he had to be finished off on the ground; as I have mentioned before, I hated this job, and always used my Browning, to the amusement of my friends. Returning at sunrise to the lodge I had to go by instinct as these parts of the forest were not well known to me, they lay far from home – about 6 miles – and I did not get there very frequently. Ivan Pavlov and his wife looked after us in a charming way, prepared tea from forest leaves – quite drinkable too – baked rye pancakes and wanted us to stay a while in their house. This suggestion touched me very much and I admired their courage, for he certainly ran risks by putting me up – the former landowner, the bourgeois, the enemy of the people – as these were the epithets we had en masse.

The same day towards evening we walked to my own place. The house was closed, the keys at the National Committee as I had preferred not to ask for them when calling for the guns. But I knew that we could stop in the cottage of my former foreman, the Tartar Ismail, a remarkable character who was so necessary to the villagers that they were sure to leave him in peace – even if they did object to my visit. He was not only the local miller now, but the only man who knew machines and their repairs, who was an agricultural expert in general and the watchmaker for many villages around.

From here, of course, I knew all my toka by heart and could even put my friend on the way to his and return to mine in good time – fortunately it was a starlit night and I could find my way. We started early, sat on one tok together to check whether it had not changed place, as I feared it might, after a railway line had been started within two miles. But the birds came all right and I shot at one with the rifle in the evening light but missed. It was obviously a very keen one who started his song before nightfall!

By 1.30 a.m. I was on my tok, having left my friend on the other. The night was ideal – not a breath of wind, a slight frost that made me shiver, the sky full of stars – and the grand silence of the sleeping forest. How I took it in and how grateful I was to live it once again. Then the first cranes called on the distant moors, and all attention was strained – I felt like I was listening with all my body. The first gurgling – then another – "good, the tok has not changed place". Then three more not far away. Time to approach the nearest. My heart thumped; I imagined noises, my imagination ran wild: what if I met someone from the village, approaching too – he'd be a poacher – not now though, the roles have reversed: I am poaching this time in the People's forest!

The cock "tokuet" (sings) lustily, he's there on one of these three pines – but on which? I go round to the song which flows rapidly, enraptured and passionate. I can't see a thing through the dark mass of healthy strong firs! I am in despair, nothing to be done but to wait until more light helps me – to hope too that the cock will go on. But suddenly a brilliant idea crosses my mind: I jump up to the stem of the pines, put my ear close to one, to the other, and hear or feel a vibration – this is where the bird is and where he sidles up and down the branch standing angrily and making the tree vibrate. I know now where to look for him, jump back for a better view – and shoot. Got him all right! There was time left for another, but then suddenly a strange noise, steps. All images of my past and present encounters with poachers surge up in my mind. I wait, the cocks stop their song – and the heavy steps? Will they stop too, waiting for the bird – or for me? No – heavy steps again, not the cautious ones of a man stalking – and there to my right, a low dark form – it is a bear as I can now discern by the gait. "Good, that's better," I feel relieved. After a short approach I had another bird and then turned for home. Strange to say the word "home". It lay there among the trees, so friendly, so dear to me, so glorious in the golden-red light of the rising sun – and lost to me.

The rest at Ismail's cottage was well earned. At dinner he told us that his boys heard villagers boasting that they had interfered with my shooting; they had probably tried to find the toka but with no result.

It was with a bit of fear, I admit, that I went to another tok the following night – took one bird and heard several shots, all haphazard in different parts of the forest, fortunately. I came back in broad daylight with the rising sun – the hares playing in the fields, sitting in a circle, bouncing crazily, chasing each other and the song of the blackcocks from their toka on forest glades and meadows – so well known to me – sounded like a triumphant awakening of life – a sound never to be forgotten. Every moment, every picture will remain to me as vivid and dear memories linked with the intimate sounds of the waking forests and fields in our colourful northern spring.

The Heather Cock's Song

Perhaps not many sportsmen have heard the spring song of the heather cock, at least I have not met many who had. In fact I always pity these people for it seems to me that they have missed at home one of the typical and most delightful songs of early spring. With us, in North Russia it was one of the most appreciated forms of shooting, with the exception of course of the capercailzie shooting during the same season, and both were called "tok", a word which can designate the actual song (with the verb being tokovat) or the place where the birds assemble for singing.

The heather cock's song has the advantage of being heard at a much greater distance and not only in the wildest parts of the forests nor only in the very early hours of the morning before sunrise, as is the case with the capercailzie. The heather cock chooses more open spaces, meadows or forest glades, starts before sunset but goes on with song and dance long after the sun has risen. Once in swing he can go on for a long time and seems untiring with his song, that is if no lady he woos pays any attention to him and of course if he is not otherwise disturbed by intruders or his own rivals.

We loved going out to watch toka on their chosen fields, generally an open forest glade, grassy and not too closed in, or a meadow on the edge of the woods with a haystack left over the winter to help the cattle out when the spring grass is still insufficient. As a rule we had huts of fir tree branches built in very early spring on these places selected by the birds for their singing contests. These huts were erected before the opening of the season so birds got used to them little by little as they turned up towards the middle of April for the singing contests. I always felt that the "tok" of the heather cocks was something like the contest of singers in Wagner's "Meistersinger", something taken very seriously by the performing individuals and probably with a final prize worthy of the best singer.

One early spring during the First World War when I was alone in Kamenka, Sasha being at the front, I decided to arrange for myself the nearest heather cock singing place or tok so as to be able to go there whenever I liked, which means on those nights when I did not go for the capercailzie, which I naturally preferred. Sidor checked up on the spot, as they often vary from year to year, and built the branch hut I had asked for. One sunny afternoon I went to have a look at the hut in daylight and to find exactly its location and arrangement: which side the entrance, how the branch door was to be opened, etc. I measured in strides the distance of the hut from the so-called Roshcha road along a ditch cutting through that field at the edge of a fir plantation. Having noted all these details I was sure to find my way also in the dark of the night and decided that I would not need Sidor, who was very busy this time of the year with work on the organisation of the timber floating. That same evening, after a nap in the armchair until about 12.30, I took my Drilling and went out without even a stable lantern for the start, counting upon finding the road which was flanked by a double row of trees for at least a mile and a half. The night was quiet and rather warm, suggesting the possibility of rain the next day. The way along the avenue and then through the Roshcha (small wood) was easy to find as I followed the ruts of the muddy road, and counting my strides from the edge of the wood I reached the ditch without difficulty, following it then across the field. It was still very dark as the sky was clouded over and I could not see much beyond two or three steps in front of me. However, by crouching low over the ground I managed to discern the outline of the hut as a black spot against the lighter sky and went straight for it across the still very slushy field. Barely had I reached it and had stretched out my hand to move the branches covering the entrance when terrific cat howl-like shrieks coming from the hut made me jump back in terror. What on earth was this? What cats can be assembled in the hut? Who could mimic cats' shrieks to frighten me? (This idea was vivid in my mind as I myself specialise in cats' cries.) At the same moment, before I had had time to answer these questions crossing my mind, a loud flutter of wings near my head startled me, and I felt a draught as wings seemed to brush my face. Birds had apparently settled on the hut for their night's rest and had scared me so much by their sudden cries that I had not recognised at first the call of the peewits. I did feel ashamed of having mistaken them at first for cats. I crept cautiously into the hut on all fours, waiting now for field mice or rats (I knew that snakes – my real terror – were not awake yet). But everything was peaceful and I settled down with my gun on my lap and the cartridge belt near me.

Very soon the first signs of dawn began to appear: grey light somewhat lighter towards the east, a slight wind which drove the clouds and cleared the sky, then ducks flew overhead, probably coming from the nearby brook and flying towards better feeding places on moor lakes, then the melodious voice of cranes rose from the distant big moors. The light was steadily growing brighter, the sun would rise soon, I thought, and at that moment I was roused out of my reverie by the close noise of wings followed by the dull thud of some heavy bird landing on the ground. I held my breath; this must be the first heather cock to arrive for the contest. I was right, for after a very few moments the cock, who must have landed very near the hut, started his song without preliminary throat clearing and grunts as is the habit of the capercailzie. This one broke out straight into its sonorous, far-reaching and melodious short song followed immediately by energetic hissing noises. I could not see the cock yet but prepared my gun in front of one of the shooting windows and waited patiently for better light. After the second or third song of this cock there came the challenging song of a rival some way away, probably among the small fir trees in the plantation. The rival was certainly on the war path for his song sounded more clearly cut, the hissing part was more prolonged and the songs followed closely one after the other. Probably mine took up the challenge, for a minute later he took to the wing and seemed to fall in very near his enemy and I waited now for the noise of a fight. As I listened intently for further developments in these quarters I was startled by the sound of wings right overhead and a big bird settled on the top of my hut. This was an unexpected prospect: I craned my neck, wishing I could turn it round in all directions like an owl, but with no result: Sidor had made such a sound waterproof top that I could not see a thing through it. At that moment my new visitor burst into song too and at such close quarters I could hear the funny little gurgling noises in his throat and a sort of tongue smacking he produced with his beak – at least this is how I explained the little noises one does not generally hear. I would never have shot this one, he was so near and was so confident that there was no hidden danger lurking from under his perch – I could not have disillusioned him. Listening to him, admiring the melodiousness of his song, the ardour of his hissing, I quite forgot my first cocks until I heard some wing-beating noises in the field which made my singer stop abruptly. Then our attention, this cock's and mine, was evidently turned in the same direction – that of the scuffle. It had got quite light by now and I could easily discern the two cocks flying at each other with anything but songs in their throats. They were magnificent as they hopped off the ground, all ruffle and bristling feathers, as they went for each other, trying to jump higher than the rival so as to attack him from above. Their black coats glistened in the early morning light, their white chests and wing linings looked whiter than snow on the dull dead green of winter grass, and their vivid red eyebrows brought an unexpected bright colour into the picture. I had always heard that the heather cock's fight is one of the most attractive and amusing sights but I had never yet witnessed one at close quarters. Of course there was no question of shooting for it was too lovely a sight, I thought, until my cock overhead got so excited that he had to join in the fray and flew off with a terrific noise of wing fluttering, probably to join the others. This was too much for me and I decided that one of the fighters must be shot or they might all decide to fly away and I would remain empty-handed. Would that matter though? Not for me, but for my prestige as a shooting woman and as the mistress of the place. So, reluctantly, I stretched out flat on the ground, took aim and shot. Fortunately I took one of the fighters as my personal friend had taken a position somewhat to the side of the fighters. The two remaining flew off as I thought towards the forest and it looked as if my morning's sport finished. I decided however, to wait before coming out of my hut as there might be some non-singing cocks, often beginners, somewhere in the bushes as well as hens which should not be unduly scared if possible. I had been right to wait and very soon two or three cocks flew up again and started their songs, mostly on the edge of the plantation where two of them chose small grassy humps as podiums and really looked lovely now in the bright low rays of the rising sun. They glistened with so many different colours for their black coat had a metallic lustre which gave the quaintest reflections in this light. Did I have to shoot them? I suppose I must, was my answer, and deciding on a compromise I loaded the rifle barrel of my Drilling and took aim at the more distant bird which had remained on lower ground, apparently keen to keep away from the fighters. The shot fell, the bird gave a quaint sudden jump, fell back on the ground, looked around with a puzzled twist of the head and then flew off following the two fighters who had been quicker in the uptake and were already on the wing. It all made me laugh: this puzzled offended look of my cock who had missed death by so little and the quick close of the singing competition. It was no use delaying any more. So I got out, glad to stretch out my limbs after crouching on the still damp ground for hours, picked up my first bird and walked home leisurely, enjoying as usual this very early spring morning with birds singing everywhere, with hares playing by the dozen in the fields, with the smoke rising straight up into the pale sky from the chimneys of the distant small village.

As I walked home and thought of my night's sport I had to recall an amusing episode which happened when I took a friend of ours to a similar heather cock "tok" or singing contest. We were in a similar hut and I let him shoot, as he rarely had an opportunity to come out. He got a cock early and could not get one near enough for a second shot until it got late and the sun was already high up in the sky. A large cock who seemed to have remained the only master of the place (the leader of the "tok" as the gamekeepers called him) had taken position on a grass hump and was singing his head off but at a distance too great for a shotgun. I suggested that my friend should take my Winchester 22 which had eleven bullets in automatic sequence and which I often carried for fancy shots, using bullets with cut off tops so as not to leave an animal wounded – if I hit at all. My friend aimed carefully and off went the first shot, the cock jumped up high, fell back on the hump and continued his song where he had broken it off (or so it seemed to me). Again a shot and no other result but another high jump, a short pause and a new song, and so it went on in a series of seven shots when I simply could not stand the strain of keeping back the laughter anymore and asked my friend to stop. He admitted that he had not given good proof of his art and we left the patient and thick-nerved cock to his love song undisturbed by the little sprays of earth raised by the bullets around him.

Tracking Hares

The first snowfall in October or November was always an exciting moment in Kamenka. The gamekeepers covered miles over their respective areas on the track of bears, looking for their winter quarters, or following the tracks of elk herds with the largest bulls. It was a general check-up of the stock of game and there was keen rivalry among the gamekeepers as to the best stock to report. If the frosts had set in before the snowfall the prospects were good: a crust of ice on the marshes and bogs would make walking easier and the first layer of snow would not melt too quickly and allow a better reading of the tracks. If there had been no frost, there would be the chance of the snow melting soon and the slush would make any progress more difficult.

Personally, I was as interested as my husband in this question of the big game, but I had also my special sport which I looked forward to very keenly. The fact is that I found immense joy in tracking hares all by myself – on foot or on skis – if there had been sufficient snow.

I remember well one October when my husband was at the front (during the First World War); we had no shooting parties in view and the gamekeepers concentrated on tracking the movements of the bears – to be tackled eventually some time later in the season. It was an ideal October: clear sunny days with a brisk light frost just enough not to harm the crops or plants (not covered yet by the protecting layer of snow) but sufficiently sharp to harden the drenched moss and peaty soil of our marshes and bogs. I was still able to ride along the meadows following the various streams or along the footpaths which always bordered the roads (riding on the road was too dangerous with the frozen clods of clay and insufficiently frozen deep ruts and holes), and was daily out in the forests where the felling had started. And then one evening it began to snow, a dry powdery snow brought by a sharp wind. By the morning the country was white – a thin, dry layer like icing sugar, just the ideal quality. I took my "Drilling", the double-barrel shotgun with a rifle barrel running underneath; a gun much if not exclusively used in Germany, hence the German name (at least this gun was little known in Russia and in France, and I think in England too). I set out with my supply of cartridges – and chocolate, which was my usual lunch when out.

My usual way lay straight through the garden, across the fields to the nearest forest where I was sure to find hares near the glades around the hay stacks. Walking was easy – I seem to tread on a carpeted floor, hard frozen soil underneath with the fresh snow deadening the sound of my steps. The sky was grey – darker towards the horizon which seemed to forecast warmer weather towards the evening. The light blanket of fresh snow was like a sheet of paper with many writings on it: the neat and dainty chain of prints left by field mice vanishing under some lump of soil, quaint patterns of small bird tracks, the large uneven ones left by crows and on the edge of the many forest the traces of many squirrels. Soon enough I came across the tracks of a hare – "Russak" – as we call the large field hare. My gun was ready with two cartridges and the bullet – in case I spied the hare outside the range of my shotgun. The field with winter corn peeping out gaily in bright green from under the light snow cover was an ideal place and I expected to find my hare lying either in the ditch or close to some bushes – digesting his early breakfast. The first thing to do was to follow the track to see the general direction chosen by the hare. Of course there were endless twists, crossing and re-crossing tracks, which made me suppose that he was near, as these manoeuvres generally start on the approaches of the selected spot. The direction led towards a slight dip in the field, a sort of gully overgrown with withered nettles and thistles. "That's the place," I thought, and decided to make a sweeping semi-circular beat to reach the opening of the gully near the forest. But, just as I had started my encircling movement I ran into the neat, mathematically even footprints of a fox! My hare is certain to have scampered away – if he was not caught – and indeed, a few yards further I saw the story written on the snow: the fox track descending in the dip following its slant on half-height, and further away the wide-set track of a hare scampering away towards the forest. No use following this one – he'll be well hidden in the bushes now and probably sleeping with open eyes.

Abandoning this field I made straight for the forest glades which were a good play ground both for the "Russak" and the "Beliak" – or white forest hare. The latter is easier game as it goes in smaller circles, is not so fast, less cautious as it is used to strange noises in the forests and, if in its winter coat already, much easier to distinguish under the trees where the snow had not penetrated yet sufficiently. Very soon I came across a maze of prints – mostly of the Beliak (smaller tracks and closer together than those of the Russak). They obviously all led into the thicket where it is a matter more of luck than of skill to follow up one particular track. However, by walking cautiously and slowly I soon managed to approach one within a bullet shot. He had already changed into his winter coat and I could see him like a white ball under the dark fir trees – his ears up – obviously scenting some danger. I levelled my gun cautiously and touched the rifle trigger. A dry shot, the hare bounced up and fell with a limp last movement of the paws. Counting my strides I went up to him – there were 80 strides – it was quite a good shot and I was pleased that the hare lay dead still as I hated to have to finish them off (for this purpose I always had my Browning with me – my friends teasing me that I want to show off my shooting hares with a revolver). It was a good start, just about lunch time too and I could enjoy my chocolate with a few cranberries to make up for anything to drink. Tying up the legs of the hare I swung him over my shoulder so as to leave my arms free and continued my sport. An hour later I spied a field hare crossing a glade that I was skirting. Difficult to approach one already on the go – rather a hopeless enterprise, unless I tried to wangle my way between the haystacks scattered on the glade. I watched and noticed soon that the hare was not scampering for shelter but seemed to be making up his mind as to which haystack was to be tackled first. He vanished behind one, then reappeared, made a semi-circle and approached it again from another side. "That's it," I thought, "he is preparing to have his meal." I let him start and then advanced very cautiously under cover of the stacks until I thought it too risky to walk up closer without leaving myself a good open range for shooting. A few more steps and the hare dashed out from behind the stack – I fired my shot and he went rolling head over heels. A second hare, and a big one too. I slung him over my shoulder – but the weight was too much for me to think of any more sport. So I turned towards home, wishing hares were not quite so heavy. It had been an ideal day, with the easy walking and the clean untouched snow and I was very pleased with the results – with the bag – yes – but especially with the clean work in reading the tracks. And I always loved to be alone when I went tracking, all my attention could centre then on the reading of the ways and habits of the animals and on the life of the forest in general. Time flew and evening always came too soon.

Volchok, the Domesticated Wolf Cub

A wolf rarely looks attractive when you see him in the zoo and there are few stories of tame wolves, even in those countries where they are to be found in large numbers. I too had always thought that they were too independent and wild to become ever really tame. But here is my true story about a wolf who was a pet.

One day, a friend rang me up from the country near Petersburg and said that he had to go away on a very long journey and asked me whether I would take his wolf cub, as my estate was not far from Petersburg either and the cub would certainly feel better there than in a town house. Of course I agreed and a few days later a gamekeeper arrived with the new pet, whose name was "Volchok" – which means "small wolf" in Russian. He was about three months old, had a brownish-greyish coat, small light eyes and a longish tail. Poor Volchok, he was terrified after the railway journey, then three hours in a sledge and then all the new faces and voices and new surroundings – too much for anyone. The gamekeeper said that the poor little cub refused to take any milk, which he usually lapped up eagerly, and would not eat anything since he left his home.

I was very worried and wondered how to get on with Volchok. The first days I did not dare pat him, for he growled and snarled, showing rows of quite impressive teeth, but he never went for anyone if left in peace. I decided to keep him in the house and to leave him alone until he got used to me and the place. A week passed and Volchok began to follow me – cautiously at first – from room to room, and even lapped his milk from the bowl when I still held it. Until then I had to put his food in some dark corner of the room and he would look at it from a distance as long as there was someone about and approach it only when he thought nobody saw him. He soon began to raise his head when I called him and even allowed a light pat. What I missed, however, was the pleasant wag of the tail which I naturally expected as he looked so much like a dog. In a month's time Volchok had become a devoted friend – at least I thought so – for he followed me patiently throughout the house and the garden, always two steps behind me; he sat at my feet during meals and ate his food wherever I gave it him. Strangely enough, he seemed to prefer being indoors and never gambolled or raced round the garden as young dogs do when they go out for a walk. He was serious, terribly serious, as if preoccupied by something, with his head low, his ears wide apart, his tail never, never wagging. When he walked his steps were slow and shuffling and sounded like an old man dragging his feet in gum boots. I could pat him now as much as I liked and he never growled, never snarled, and even pressed his head against my knee evidently pleased and quite happy at the moment. He was growing rapidly and his coat had become softer and more of a dusty colour.

Volchok was really quite clever by now and very attentive to everything that happened round him. He knew, for instance, that in the evening when I went upstairs to my bedroom he could not go up with me; he knew that when I went out riding he had to stay at home; he was always clean in the house and never tried to gnaw or tear books or boots, or eat the best felt hat to be found in the hall – as puppies generally do. He never played with anything and remained indifferent to people coming in and out of the house. But he invariably followed me everywhere (except to the stables where the horses snorted and became restless), and he lay at my feet when I read or worked, looking up attentively at the least noise or movement – and he never barked. I really did not know his voice and this always puzzled me and seemed to me unnatural. What worried me, however, was that he did not seem to pay attention to anyone else but me and that no one could pat him without getting a snarl in reply. He did know, though, the head gamekeeper who looked after him when I was away for a few days, but he remained sulky and quiet in his corner and refused to move, eating very little until I returned.

Months passed. I had to spend some time in my town house and sulky Volchok, sad and unapproachable when without me, had to be left in the country. At the time my little boy, aged three, was just beginning to take an interest in animals and insisted on petting them, and Volchok was of course a great attraction. But his answers to the little boy's pats were too dangerous and I was very little certain how far the little boy and the little wolf would always obey the nurse. Things could not go on like that – it was too dangerous and it was with the greatest regret and sorrow that I was finally obliged to give Volchok to the zoo. I knew he would be well looked after but it was sad to send away such a devoted and quiet friend. I could not see him go and left for Petersburg the day before he was brought away.

I called once at the zoo some weeks later, but it was too sad to see him there, to see his small light eyes look fixedly at me – as if asking a question. I never went there again.

Filka, the Decoy Owl

Filka had a great fascination for me. He was a huge eagle owl over two foot high with magnificent golden-brown plumage and lovely transparent eyes. He had been caught on the estate years before I met him. The story went that he was the largest of his kind ever seen in the local forests and several offers to buy him had been made to the estate manager. But Filka was too beautiful to be parted with and remained thus an honoured inhabitant of Kamenka. However, he was far from being a pet and I often wondered whether it ever would be possible to make a pet out of this impressive and proud old gentleman. He really seemed to deserve the name he bears in French – *hibou grand-duc*. Never had I seen one like him, with so much dignity, aloofness and such a self-possessed expression of set ill humour. To me, at least, he appeared to be always ill-humoured and ready to utter some unpleasant sound to express hurt dignity and profound disapproval. And Filka must have disapproved of me highly, I am sure, for I was the only person who came up to his cage daily and who never brought him anything as I did not know his taste. My visits were pure, blank, ill-mannered curiosity and no wonder that he disapproved of them. At first I could not understand the reason of his curses but at last I did understand and tried then to find something to offer him. Unfortunately his favourite dishes were not exactly appetising: dead mice, rats, moles and skinned squirrels. To obtain these unprepossessing morsels I had to ask Sidor, the gamekeeper in charge of Filka, or a stable boy or someone on the farm; all were helpful in providing Filka's daily fare. Finally I dropped all hesitation about taking up a sport which was not considered at the time as quite suitable for the lady of the house, and armed with my small Winchester rifle I started looking myself for Filka's special game. What the household thought of me I don't know. In their eyes it was bad enough that I went shooting with my husband and his friends, but to shoot mice and rats on the farm must have seemed quite disreputable.

But back to Filka. He sat erect and ponderous in his large cage in an outhouse near the stables waiting for his dinner, always ready for a bite. I was rather scared at first when handing it to him through the bars of the cage, for his talons looked terribly impressive and the way he suddenly stretched out his foot was so strange and swift and so totally out of keeping with his usual immobility and stately demeanour. It was a flash-like sudden thrust of a terrifying dark foot accompanied by a rapid, ferocious blinking of the huge golden-brown, nearly orange eyes. Often he made a funny little chuckling noise and I hoped it was an expression of satisfaction, but I doubt it, for I heard it again later, in May or June, when he was taken out of the cage for the shooting and I don't think he particularly liked being disturbed.

This shooting with Filka became one of my favourite sports during an otherwise dead season. Sidor erected in various places on the open fields low branch huts with a six-foot pole driven into the earth a couple of yards from each. These poles had a short crossbar on the top fixed loosely and with a spring connecting one end of it with the pole about two feet below the top. A long rope leading from the hut was fixed to the other end of the bar with the result that when the rope was pulled, the crossbar bent down but immediately jerked back into position. Filka, brought in a special basket that Sidor carried on his back, was set on to the crossbar, and the chain fixed to his foot was clipped to a ring on the bar. We then crept into the hut with our shotguns and our watch began.

Though dignified as usual, Filka lost some of his aloofness. Perhaps the sunshine disturbed him or the smell of the fields, the song of the larks roused him out of his indifference. Perhaps it was simply the excitement at the change of his surroundings. He began by sidling along the bar in one direction and then the other, then he shook himself violently whereby his lovely plumage shone in the sun in the warmest copper and golden tints. Finally he settled down quietly, but if he looked like musing in the way a wise old man should muse we tugged the rope slightly to make him lose his balance. He then fluttered frantically and his wide-spread wings beat the air in sweeping gestures. This sudden movement attracted the attention of sparrow hawks, buzzards, goshawks and other birds of prey. It was fascinating to see Filka get excited long before we ourselves heard or sighted any of these enemies; he would ruffle his feathers, sidle along the bar and finally, when we could already hear the whooshing sound of a buzzard soaring above us, Filka started to turn his head, following the sound, and it looked absolutely as if he could turn it right round, like a doll's head on a loose neck. His eyes blinked fast, his whiskers moved up and down and the head thrown back looked straight up from above his ruffled neck. Then came a whistling sound, a flash above Filka, who beat the air furiously with outspread wings, drawing his neck into his shoulders and uttering funny guttural sounds, just as the buzzard or hawk pounced down towards him. And here we came into the picture. Peering between the branches we shot either when the bird was just approaching Filka – this was the right moment – or just after it had swept past him. This latter shot, however, was less advisable. How many times I missed at first! Petrified for fear of hitting Filka and too fascinated by his entice, I was too slow for the sudden swoop. It was good practice for fast shooting, at which my husband was extremely good, but I had first to learn the necessary concentration and patience and learn not to be distracted by Filka's funny ways and sounds.

We never returned empty-handed from these shooting expeditions and it was always interesting to examine the bag. I wondered at the number and variety of birds of prey that used to fly overhead, at the difference in the size of males and females of some species, at the rich colouring of some. Once my husband shot a remarkably well-marked spotted eagle, another time an osprey, both rarely seen in our parts; they were duly stuffed to occupy an honoured place in the hall. I have heard of rooks, ravens and crows being attracted by stuffed owls used as bait but I never had the opportunity of shooting any with Filka and I presume that the presence of larger birds of prey frightened away the more modest birds.

Poor Filka used to look tired after the excitement of these attacks which gave us so much selfish pleasure, and when Sidor put him back into his travelling basket Filka seemed to enter it quite willingly and was docile, not vicious as he had been at the start. The next few days he looked drowsy and sleepy, his fare being more abundant than usual since he ate with gusto his fallen enemies. When I called on him he blinked lazily and did not use

95

the aggressive language he usually did, so I decided that a good meal makes even an owl quite benevolent.

Smoliakov, the Drunken Odd Job Man

If a man was wanted for any odd job in the farm, in the garden, or even in the house, invariably the choice would fall upon Smoliakov. Invariably, too, the job would come to a premature end because Smoliakov would either get dead drunk as soon as he could lay his hands on a few coins – or better still on bottles of wine – or then he'd be caught carrying away something from the house or the garden to exchange it for vodka. However, it would likely be he again who would be called in when odd help was needed next time.

He was always available, being desperately lazy and having an excellent and energetic wife who managed his little farm independently from him. When not drunk Smoliakov could be found either lying on his stove (the Russian village houses have large stone stoves with a kind of terrace on the top) smoking abominable cigarettes, or hammering leisurely about in a corner of his yard. His goat-like face with the thin yellow beard and pale blue eyes was always smiling a somewhat cunning smile, and his conversation would be illustrated by a series of jokes, quite clever though generally risqué.

My husband had a weakness for Smoliakov and forgave him easily his crimes. As for me, I was fascinated by his amusing ways and his versatile behaviour. Outside, in the kitchen, in the pantry, he would be the ideal model of comfortable laziness; in our house, in the masters' rooms, he suddenly became the most active and busy man, shuffling about in his soft felt boots doubled up with politeness, craning his neck, his meagre beard shaking with officiousness. Only his eyes remained the same, always laughing at us, at himself, at life? Who knows?

His face was a study when he sighted vodka knowing that he'd get some. Eyes, nose, beard, all became pointed as if attracted with equal force by the beloved liquid. I always believed his ears turned in the same direction but I am not sure that I actually saw it. My husband was selfish enough to give the man a drink for the mere sake of seeing this expression, and the slow, almost penetrated movement with which he approached the glass to his lips and emptied it then with a jerk into his mouth.

However, even the indulgence of my husband could not endure the too-free impulsiveness of Smoliakov when drink was concerned. No bottles in the house were safe from him – he seemed to penetrate everywhere.

Once, on a very thirsty day of his, he was caught as he was rushing off to the village inn, his pockets bulging with teacups. When stopped and asked for an explanation, he replied, smiling gently, "Excuse, my Lady, I am so sorry. I made a mistake and took the cups from the wrong set." This is all he could find in explanation of his strange behaviour.

When beaters were wanted for our shoots, Smoliakov would be the first to appear on the spot, his high felt boots filled with hay at the top to prevent the snow from falling in. He acted as if ready to take the lead of the beaters, evidently knowing well that he would be entrusted with his favourite task – watching over the sledges which had brought us to the shoot. The beaming smile, the repeated nods and the cunning expression of the eyes made me always suspect that he enjoyed in advance the idea of cuddling up in our fur coats we used for driving and generally left in the sledges when going to the stands. He had apparently taken a preference for my squirrel-lined coat out of which he scampered always a second too late when we were returning to the sledges – and the smell of this poor coat after the service it had rendered him should better remain undescribed.

The news of his death from his widow made a deep impression upon me.

We met her one day on the road, just after having returned from a prolonged stay in town. She bowed low before us and, wiping her eyes with the corner of her broad apron, said, "The Lord has called away my Smoliak, my Lady; I am left a widow."

When I expressed my regret and asked whether he had been ill, she told me with a tear-stained face, "My Smoliak has never been ill. He just began to feel weaker and weaker and his eyes looked further beyond; and one day he came down from the stove, told me to arrange a couch on the bench under the icons, as he was going to die. So he lay there for a day without saying a word but muttering prayers and then, towards evening, he turned to me saying, 'Katerina, it's coming, good-bye,' and never breathed again."

A simple and quiet death lighting up the figure of an old drunkard.

Izmail, the Handyman

"Izmail must do this, Izmail will know how to fix that . . ." was the first thing to say when something went wrong in the house or on the farm in Kamenka. And this is too what I thought when I had some new idea about improvements to be made. Lost as we were among endless forests, some thirty miles from the nearest larger village, post and the railway station of Tosno, we really needed a man who had imagination and could see to things. And in fact, Izmail *could* do things and was never as happy as when he had some unusual task put before him. To fix some new equipment in the mill, to build a greenhouse, to grow some unusual vegetables, to lay on water in the cowsheds or put up a new bathroom in the house – for all these and many other tasks Izmail always found time, was always eager, keen and resourceful.

Small, wiry, with dark eyes, high cheek bones and a fine set mouth, Izmail, a Tartar, was very different from our northern peasant. He was born near the Ural where my husband had inherited a large estate when still a small boy. Izmail, a young boy too, had first played with the new little master, then had accompanied him on his rides and hunts and had become his devoted companion. His eyes were as sharp as those of a falcon, he could spot the falling game far in the fields, he could run as fast as a dog to pick up the wounded bird or hare – the master and the little Tartar had become inseparable, spending the summer weeks together roaming about the endless fields with the Urals on the horizon.

Then my husband, as a young man already, sold this estate and Izmail decided to follow his master and came to the northern estate where he remained until the end – until the revolution in 1917/18 deprived us of all our possessions.

It was during the war of 1914–18 that I first knew how to appreciate Izmail. He was not mobilised, having a weak chest, and remained as foreman on the estate farm of Kamenka. My husband, the estate manager and several men on the farm left for the army at the outbreak of the war and I really don't know what I would have done without Izmail, as the management of the estate fell on my shoulders and I had absolutely no previous experience and was still very young. But Izmail was always on the ball, he never hesitated and he ran the farm so efficiently and well that I never had any trouble or great difficulties. We discussed matters together, for he never took any steps without referring to me first, but I knew he was doing his best and it seemed to work. Fortunately, I was thus left free to run the extensive and important side of the estate – the forests with the annual felling, lumbering, afforestation and drainage.

Izmail's position was not easy, for a Tartar and non-Christian was not easily accepted as a head to be obeyed. But somehow he succeeded in making himself generally respected, if not exactly loved – I think his quick temper blazing up into regular rages frightened our more placid northerners and they kept out of his way for the sake of peace.

He had the reputation of being fearless – what this reputation was based on I don't know, but he had to live up to it, and in fact it was he alone who could tackle the fierce bull we had at the time, and it was he alone who could coax my really dangerous Caucasian wolf hound, Topka, into returning to his kennel when he got loose by accident and the whole village ran for shelter on hearing that he was at liberty.

My eldest two boys had the greatest respect for Izmail, a little awe too, I think, for he never spoke much nor played with them but quietly answered their questions, put in a little joke and never allowed them to interfere on the farm or with the agricultural machines, which were always an attraction to boys. But I knew he had an eye on them and I could rely upon him in an emergency. A little incident confirming these feelings remains well engraved in my memory. One autumn evening, returning home after an absence of two days in Petersburg, I found Izmail waiting for me at the gate – an unusual place for him to be.

I stopped the carriage and asked him anxiously what had happened, for there had been rumours of robbers roaming about the country and I only left the house reluctantly on urgent business.

"Everything is all right, my Lady – only I wanted to warn my Lady about master Vladimir. He is all right, but there might be some difficulties about him and I just wanted to say that he is all right – and a nice straight boy too."

This puzzled me but I did not pose any questions, just thanked Izmail, feeling quite certain that there was something where I'd have to be careful in judging the boy – a bit of a handful at the time. How thankful I was for this timely warning when approaching the boy the next day. Had I only listened to the accounts of his governess and nurse I certainly would have adopted the wrong attitude. But with Izmail's words ringing in my ears I soon came to an understanding with the boy. In fact, exasperated by these governesses during my absence, he had run away early in the morning having decided to join his father at the front, but hungry and cold by the end of the day he returned at sunset, staging a swoon – apparently staging it extremely well – only to cover his failure and to give his governesses "a good fright" as they had "bored him stiff" – which I well believe in spite of all their excellent qualities. The boy had simply outgrown them and wanted a man's hand to guide him. And Izmail had understood and the boy, reviving from his swoon, would not speak with anyone but him.

With an inquisitive brain and very deft hands, Izmail had learnt to repair watches and soon became the watchmaker of the district. In early spring he was overburdened with work and sat up late into the night repairing the watches and clocks for all the peasants who came down from villages scores of miles away, following the stream with the floating timber on high water, to return upstream a few weeks later.

Izmail was also our miller and mechanic for all agricultural machines. When a strategic railway line was being built through our estate in 1915, Izmail and I sat for hours over catalogues and books learning the works of a sawing mill, because I found out that sawing boards on the spot would be most advantageous. A few weeks later our old locomobile puffed cheerfully away at the end of the park, running now not only the mill but also a brand new sawing mill.

Another of Izmail's hobbies was photography and some of the best pictures he took are still to be found in the *Illustrated London News* of 1912. I lost all my photographs, having to leave them in Russia, and was happy to find in England, twenty years later, a copy of this special Russian number with Izmail's photographs in it.

There was one great problem in his life: he was a Tartar and a Mahommedan and no Russian priest could marry him to the Russian girl who had joined him from the Ural estate. When his first son was born, Izmail asked me to be his godmother, to which I willingly agreed much to the indignation of the villagers and servants but to the great satisfaction of the kind red-bearded priest.

When with the revolution we were deprived of our estates, houses and capital and I tried in vain to get out of the country, Izmail frequently came up to town in spite of the long journey and brought me what he could spare: a little rye flour, some potatoes, dry mushrooms or vegetables. Being the miller and the only expert with agricultural machines, he had been left in peace in the cottage on the estate and could carry on his work. It is to him that I came, on foot, when I felt like seeing the old home which, though "nationalised", had not been definitely taken from me but where I could not stay alone. Izmail and Katia did their best to make me comfortable in their cottage and they were not afraid of the local communists who might object to my coming – the "former landowner".

Michailo and the Pork Chops

Michailo was one of our younger gamekeepers who had been taken on when some of the older ones were called up at the outbreak of the war. As an only son he was not subject to military service (at least not at the beginning) and was glad to have a job which did not take him from his village where his widowed, half-blind mother could not look after the cottage and the strip of land they had alone.

Michailo knew nothing about game and shooting and looked at the older gamekeepers with large brown inquiring eyes when they explained in a whisper how the beaters were to be led, where they were to start, etc. And I was convinced that Michailo never understood the complicated strategic plans and that the old beaters did the job perfectly well by themselves. Still, Michailo got his jacket with the proper buttons and the green edge and reported to me on the appointed days. What he reported – when it meant tracks of elk or lynx – always remained extremely vague, and after listening patiently to his story I looked at the district map, gathered what I could and then called the head gamekeeper, Sidor, to hear his opinion, but never gave away Michailo with his vague description. Sidor knew, of course, everything – as he always did in general – and if a shoot was to take place he would organise things and Michailo followed conscientiously the instruction he received. Thus Michailo got on all right, smiled, obeyed and remained as vague as ever. I noticed that when leading the beaters he always lagged behind and when told to carry the guns he held them so clumsily and gave them such plaintive, furtive looks as if he expected them to shoot off by themselves. Michailo became a sort of joke among the men on the farm who called him "Michailo the courageous".

When the revolution broke out Michailo's face acquired a new, still more frightened expression for which I could not account at first. He still turned up for his regular weekly reports but only towards evening and several times I asked him why he chose this time as he would reach home only in the dark. Turning his cap in his hand, pushing his hair off his forehead, he replied in an uneasy tone that he did not mind getting home in the dark, that he had had some job on hand at home, etc. I felt that the man was ill at ease and asked Sidor one day what was happening to Michailo to make him so uneasy. Sidor mumbled something, looked uneasy too and shrugging his shoulders said, "Well, Madam, Michailo is not courageous you know, and he is worse now." I saw there was nothing to be got out of him either and really abandoned the matter. Time went by. The revolution grew. Nearly a year after its outbreak our Kamenka was taken from us. Life in Petersburg became more and more difficult; food was scarce. We lived on rye flour, on pumpkins, there was no butter, no fat whatsoever; people exchanged carpets, clothes, any household articles for a little food, which could only be got underhand and at great risks for both bargaining sides. I was fortunate enough to have always some rye flour, sometimes some potatoes, which were a luxury. Rye flour or potatoes were boiled as it was the only way they could be prepared. My old servants from Kamenka, the coachman Ivan, the foreman Izmail, the gamekeepers Ivan Ivanovich or Ivan Pavlovich, always managed to bring me the flour or the potatoes so that I never really went hungry. I appreciated the more the devotion of these men for it meant a long trip for them, a day's journey at times, when the roads were bad or when they had to walk all the way to the station, some twenty miles and more.

One November morning in 1919 my maid, who still lived in my house, to my great relief, came to me to announce the arrival of a man who said he came from Kamenka but whom she did not know. I asked her to bring him in, wondering who it could be and rather dreading some Bolshevik messenger on an obviously unpleasant errand. What was my surprise when I saw Michailo appear at the door, smiling shyly, twiddling his cap as usual.

"Michailo, how nice to see you. How goes life with you?"

"Very well, Madam, mother is all right too. Here is a little present for you with our greetings," and he tended me a parcel wrapped in brown paper.

"Thank you Michailo, but what can it be?" I answered, very puzzled.

"You see, we had to kill our pig as neighbours were casting ugly glances at us for still having a pig. So we thought you might like some chops and – they are fresh for I left home last night late. It took me some time to find your street, I don't know the town," he added with an apologetic smile.

"Oh, you must be very tired, Michailo, this is so kind of you to have taken all this trouble. It will be delightful to have pork chops – I have not seen meat for weeks – it will be a great feast, thank you. But you must rest, Michailo, have a good sleep tonight and go back tomorrow morning."

"No, Madam, this won't do. I must go soon and be on my way from the station when it gets dark . . ." and as he noticed my astonished look, he added, "Times have changed, our people are not as they were . . . if they guessed I was going to you . . . bringing this present to you . . . well, one never knows . . . better return in the dark."

Poor Michailo, teased for being a bit of a coward. How hard it must have been for him to overcome all his fears and to undertake the long trip with two sleepless nights. I suddenly realised it all – and good Michailo became very dear to me.

As to the chops – they made the joy of two old friends of mine: one a tiny little woman full of energy and resourcefulness, the other a huge good-natured man who loved his food and who had had to live now on a pumpkin menu for weeks . . .

LOUISINO

7

WOLVES

Wolves I: Hunting Wolves with Borzois

Besides our gun dogs we also kept a pack of borzoi hounds at Louisino. We had twelve of them; they had been given us by the Grand Duke Nicholas from his famous kennels. They were used for hunting wolves in the autumn, when the presence of wolves began to make itself felt. The wolves became more audacious at this time of year, and rumours would reach us from the villages that calves and foals had disappeared while grazing in the harvested fields or in the wooded valleys.

Pictures and descriptions generally connect wolves with a wintry landscape, with masses of snow and big forests. It is true that the wolf looks his best in winter when his coat is thick and fluffy, when its colours are vivid and well marked, when walking through the deep snow makes him carry his head high and forces him to adopt a lighter gait as he could not shuffle his feet through the snow or plough it with a low bent head. Besides, it is difficult to see him in summer when he hides during daylight in the thickets and bushes and may be noticed only towards evening, as a shadow stealthily crossing a glade or slipping back into the forest if disturbed in his stalking sheep or calves. However, when hunted by borzois (the Russian long-haired greyhound) the wolf does make a good picture of strength and of swift action. As this kind of hunting takes place on the flat, in the steppes – where fields stretch out for miles and miles without a break, without a hedge, without a ditch, often without even the row of trees marking a road – there is ample time to admire both the wolf and the work of the dogs as you gallop after them. The borzois are keen sporting dogs, but contrary to all other dogs they rely exclusively on their eyesight, which is remarkable, and they simply have no scent at all. They are so passionate in their pursuit of the game that they are apt to run head forward into a hedge or a tree or any similar obstacle, and the impact is so strong that they can be killed on the spot. This is why all hunting with borzois can be done only in flat and free country. They dash after anything that runs and often you find them off after a small village dog just as eagerly as if it were a hare, a fox or a wolf. This is why they are mostly kept in kennels and taken out only on the leash for the sport.

I remember in particular one day which turned out to be eventful in the series of hunts with these dogs. In fact, the events were not important, but they marked the day. Firstly, our estate manager lost his galosh; secondly, our best rider was pulled clear off his horse by his own dogs; and thirdly, we took a big, old wolf who had been the terror of the village herds for miles around. We set out rather late that morning on a dull and damp autumn day. It had been raining hard throughout the night and we wondered whether it would be worthwhile hunting as the wolves would probably keep close to the thicket, unwilling to venture out far. However, it cleared up and by nine o'clock we were on our horses, four riders and two or three borzois with each. The borzois, tall and slender with their long silken coats of fawn, black and white or fawn and black, looked eager with their small ears slightly cocked up, their heads high, their eyes attentive and keen. Large iron rings in their collars allow for an easy movement of the long leash which passes through the rings of three dogs at a time, or of a couple. Single borzois are rarely used. Both ends of the leash are held by the rider, one end can be fixed to the arm of the rider but the other must lie loosely in his hand, for at any given moment he must let it go instantaneously or else run the risk of being swept clear off his mount by the simultaneous dash of his two or three borzois, should they spy the game before their master.

We set out in good order with two gamekeepers holding a couple of hounds which were to help us detect the wolves in the groups of brushwood scattered here and there among the fields.

The soil was still sloshy and sticky. We came near a small island of brushwood where wolves and foxes often took cover, and as we were taking our stands round it I noticed the absence of our estate manager, an excellent shot and a good huntsman in general but a very poor rider. There he was, some way behind us, turning his horse right and left, backwards and forwards, making his dogs evidently nervous as he pulled their leash in all directions. "Pavel Ivanovich, what are you doing there? Have you lost something?" I asked him, riding up to him in haste and noticing that he bent low over the saddle, evidently looking for something on the ground. He looked up, reddened, his short-sighted eyes blinking through his very thick glasses. "So sorry to delay you, but I have lost my galosh."

"Your galosh? Why? You ride in galoshes?" and I noticed a glossy rubber galosh on his left riding boot.

"Yes ... no ... you see I get off the horse so often when I don't want to, and it has been raining all night – I thought it would be reasonable . . ." and he did not finish his sentence.

"Come along, come along," I said, turning away hastily to conceal a smile that I could not suppress, "We are taking this island now. Afanasii (a gamekeeper) can look for the galosh later."

"Thank you, that's all right," and Pavel Ivanovich followed me to our stands. I think the galosh was found the next day – full of water, I fear, as it rained hard all night.

The dogs went through the island, no trace of game, apparently, and we met again, the men to smoke a cigarette while the gamekeepers led the dogs along the stretch of unknown grass and thistles adjoining the island. Our friend, a cavalry officer and excellent rider, had twisted the loose end of his leash round his wrist now and I warned him timidly for he was a good huntsman and I did not dare give him a warning. He laughed good naturedly, "I'll always have time to let go if necessary – see the dogs are bored, there is no game near evidently." He bent down over the closely clasped hands trying to light a cigarette in the strong wind and a second later he was down flat on his stomach, his borzois wrestling themselves free from the leash just as I, more or less instinctively, let go the loose end of mine to give free scope to my three borzois. The hounds were giving voice, the gamekeepers called, and in a flash I saw the shape of a large wolf emerge from the far end of the row of thistles and behind him my three borzois followed by the two of our friend. This was stupid, I thought, for my three work well together and I wonder whether the others won't interfere with them. The wolf was gaining ground and making straight for the forest on the horizon. A good run to there, that was good, and as we all followed at full gallop the distance between us and the wolf seemed to diminish slightly. My three borzois were leading now and I could already make out their tactics: the two on the flanks were redoubling their efforts, bending like a tightened bow to straighten themselves out like a dart a second later – a lovely sight. The centre one continued in the same even and steady pace, methodical, sure, undisturbed. There, the flank borzois are now on a level with the wolf – they even seem to pass him – when, as if following some unseen signal, they suddenly both turn sharp towards the wolf and pounce upon him simultaneously from right and left, whereas the centre one, dashing forward with sudden keenness, comes up from the rear and buries his teeth in the back of the wolf's neck, the flank ones hold the prey on both sides. The animals topple over in a bundle, roll over – and stop. It is suddenly quiet and I turn away. It was a lovely sight and an exhilarating gallop, but I was sorry for the wolf. Panting and wagging their feathery tails, my three borzois come up to me for praise – they worked well and deserve the praise. The side glance they throw to their two competitors who came late made me think of rather poor sportsmen glad to show off. The wolf was a big animal – probably the terror of the village – and we were glad to have got him. I was proud of the excellent teamwork of my dogs, but sorry for our friend, the cavalry officer, whose dogs had tried gallantly to do their best but who – not having been released in time – had wasted a few precious seconds. Besides, he himself did not see the joke of his fall and had so many excuses and explanations to give that we never dared tease him about it. As for Pavel Ivanovich – he managed to stay on his horse throughout the day and only on the way home suddenly came down when his horse, recognising stable companions in an adjacent field, made a rather unexpected thrust to the left. The lonely galosh thus came in useful in the end.

Wolves II: Family Behaviour

We were in our country place not far from Kursk where the steppes begin and the last large forests stretch out in green and brown patches among the endless flat fields. The weather was perfect – warm September sunshine and cool refreshing nights. At dawn every day we went out shooting – ducks, snipe, grouse – and every evening when we came home we heard a new story about wolves having carried away sheep, calves and even foals from the village herds. The horses and the cattle spent the nights in the fields guarded by small boys only, and the wolves attacked the young stock and carried away their prey into the neighbouring forests, which belonged to us. Finally, the wolves became so daring that they penetrated into the village in the night, broke into the courtyard of a farm and carried away several of the sheep herded there in an enclosure. The villagers asked us to help them destroy these raiders.

Before organising a hunt with beaters and dogs we had to make sure in which part of the forest these wolves had their lairs. Thus after sunset we drove off to the forest, taking an old horse which would not be nervous of wolves and fastening it to a tree on a glade, and one of the two men, an experienced hunter, began to howl most dismally, imitating the voice of the old wolf. It was something like a dog howling at the moon, only more wailing, more dismal and intensely sad. I knelt, the gun in my hands, listening intently. There, from the right, came an answer, a howl somewhat different, shorter, quicker. "This is the mother answering," murmured the huntsman, and there came suddenly from the left now an excited choir of thin impatient howls – evidently the children calling the mother. The huntsman now stopped his call and told me to look sharply across the moonlit glade as the mother wolf may very possibly come this way hurrying to her children. There again the call of the mother, nearer this time, and close to her another voice, one that I had not heard yet and that I mistook for the whining of a young dog. The huntsman leaned over to me and murmured, "This is her last year's pup, one of them frequently remains near the mother even when she has another family. Look out for them, they may cross here together, shoot either of them." No, I thought, I won't shoot the yearling – even the mother? How can I when she hastens to the waiting children? No, I would hate to do it – and I hope they won't come across here. Just as these thoughts crossed my mind our old horse snorted and moved restlessly about. Evidently the wolves were near and, however old and quiet, the horse did not like them. Dear old horse – and there a dark speck disappearing in the shade of the hazelnut thicket on the right. "Bad luck, the stupid horse has frightened them away," murmured the huntsman, "They won't come here again, but we know where the brood is." A quarter of an hour later we were leaving the forest and, as we stopped at the edge to find the shallow place to cross the ditch, we heard in the distance the long and dismal wailing and howl – exactly like the voice of our huntsman. It was the father wolf probably coming home to his family and announcing his arrival to them – with prey or not – I could not tell.

Wolves III: The Lair

A few days after having discovered the whereabouts of the wolves' lair we set out one morning to shoot them – full of the best intentions but with very little hope of success. We were only four guns, the local foresters knew little of the game (they had not even been poachers in private life), their four or five dogs of non-descript breeds looked none too obedient as they snarled ferociously at each other and altogether we were too few people for the large district of forests and adjacent fields which had to be combed through. As it was the end of the harvest everyone was busy and friends on the neighbouring estates could not be contacted in time because of the big distances, absence of telephones and unreliable postal service.

The day was magnificent – a real joy to be out in the forest, all golden, brown and green with autumn colours. We roamed about, the dogs roamed on their own paying very little attention to their masters' orders; each forester knew the best way and the best moment to encircle the wolves, while the wolves were clever enough to dodge us all without much difficulty, I suppose. The absence of a proper organisation of trained gamekeepers and dogs was felt from the start. We knew from the beginning what we were to expect as this estate was run by an elderly lady who had neither interest nor understanding for sport. Thus the day was spent in running to and fro in the forest in vain attempts to follow the voices of the dogs, each of them hunting on his own, and in casual meetings on some clearing for a cigarette and a chat.

After a good lunch on a forest glade, when men and dogs felt lazy and ready for a nap, I went off on my own as I knew the glade and remembered well the direction from which the whole family of baby wolves had called their mother a few nights before. I set out in that direction and soon found that the undergrowth of the forest became thicker and thicker, that the high grass grew coarser and higher and that the paths trodden down by the cattle that grazed on and around the glade disappeared entirely. With difficulty I pushed my way through the thicket and soon felt a quaint and unpleasant smell that became steadily stronger and more distinct. There was no doubt: the smell, unpleasant and penetrating, must come from the lairs and, like a dog sniffing a top scent, I advanced now trusting only my nose as I could not see where I went. A path reappeared suddenly and as I looked closer I noticed that there were only traces of wolves on it, no human footprints. This is the wolves' track leading to the lair and the lair must be pretty near now, I thought, as the track was well trodden down and the smell had become extremely unpleasant. Still, I advanced, holding my loaded gun level and ready to shoot, stopping very frequently to listen whether any sound of the animals could be discerned in the stillness of the forest. Somewhere, very far, I could hear the faint voice of one of our dogs but otherwise not a sound. Suddenly I saw light in front of me, a patch of brilliant sunshine on an apparent opening. And the smell – it was appalling now. As I stepped out of the thicket into the light I saw in front of me a real litter of bones, skulls of animals, rags of hides – evidently this was the dining room of the wolves' family and these were the remainders of the great feasts held here daily or nightly – on the village cattle. The grass was stamped down everywhere, the lower branches of the surrounding bushes were partly broken, partly bent, and numerous tracks, large and small, led in all directions.

Apparently this was not only the dining room but also the play room of the wolf family, and I quite expected now to meet the children in their night nursery. The idea of meeting their mother was perhaps not quite as pleasant and I grasped my gun more firmly and listened more cautiously to any suspicious noise. But it was still, completely silent all round me; a few big flies were buzzing over the bones – that was all. Since I have come so far I must see the night nursery, I thought, but how unpleasant it was now to bend low under the branches of the thick bushes over these trodden-down and bone-strewn tracks. Evidently the young wolves have the same habit as puppies – namely to carry away the best piece and to eat it somewhere in seclusion, unseen by the others. Barely a few yards further I came to another smaller glade, in fact only a small round space between the bushes, a thick layer of dry grass like a litter, a close wall of bushes and high, reed-like, sharp-bladed grass all round. This is the real lair, the nursery – and no one at home. I was disappointed, although I knew that the family must be old enough at this time of the year to run quite a few miles behind the mother, and our roaming about in the forest all day would evidently send the family far away. As I stood there looking at this cosy little nursery and imagining the fluffy wolves playing about on the good and soft litter, I heard the faint sound of the hunters' horn blowing the "join up" signal. I guessed that it was intended for me as my companions would probably wonder what had become of me. The sun was low now, its red and golden rays cut sharp slanting lines into the thicket. I turned round and wound my way back through bushes and grass, due west as I remembered having come from that direction. Half an hour later, still in the thicket, I heard pattering feet, sniffing – "Is it the family coming home?" I thought, and once again assured myself by readying my gun. Then a few bounds, tail-beating on bushes – our dogs, and behind them one of my companions quite cross and angry.

"Where have you disappeared? Have you lost your way that you got into this thicket?"

"No, I went to look for the lair of the wolf family and I have found it – but it is empty."

"The lair? You are crazy to go there alone – a nice greeting you might have had there."

114

I did not answer but I thought little about the greeting and was glad I had seen the home of the wolves and had found it myself, alone, for the sound of human voices did not suit the place and might have disturbed the owners – if they were anyway near. The hunters were tired and a little glum – the bag of the long day was but a brace of hares. The villagers will be disappointed and distressed. But I was pleased with the day's experience and quite happy that the family of wolves remained untouched – albeit a little disturbed, I fear.

Hunting Wolves with Beaters and Red Flags

Snowdrifts are always a nuisance, especially when you have made up your mind to hunt wolves and to do it in the "classical way" of the season – that is with beaters and red rags. These snowdrifts are bad enough in the north of Russia, but at least here the dense forests and thickets of fir trees break the force of the wind and offer some shelter to man and beast. In the south, however, in the steppes and the regions bordering the steppes, the gaunt branches of the leafless trees offer but little protection from the snow and wind, which sweep over the country unhindered.

One January, when we had gone down south to the Louisino estate with the object of shooting wolves there in the "classical" way, the snowdrifts never stopped and the snow came down in masses day and night, the thermometer going lower and lower – nearly as far as the scale allowed it – and the efforts of the gamekeeper to trace the wolves and to ascertain where they had their favourite hunting grounds remained unsuccessful. All traces of man and beast were immediately covered by a soft and uniform layer of fresh snow, all roads were levelled out with the surrounding fields; the villages were like islands in a sea of snow. Only the small peasant horses managed to plough their way through, pulling the flat, broad sledges which swayed and dived like flat-bottomed boats. Afanassi, the gamekeeper, was in utter despair and we were already giving up all hope of ever sighting a wolf this season. And then, one morning, the sun was shining, the sky was blue and it was intensely cold. Afanassi had left at dawn on his skis to look for the wolves, whose traces would be seen now as if traced on a map of snow. By noon he was back with the good news that four wolves were for certain in the northern end of the forest and that by two o'clock we, the guns, should be there. He immediately took the beaters and the red rags to encircle the beat before our arrival.

It took us nearly an hour to get to the indicated spot, which was only some three miles away but the horses could barely make their way through the masses of fresh snow. The sledges trailed on the soft surface and there was no trace of beaten track anywhere. The sun was brilliant, the shadows of our sledges blue, as if transparent and distant. No time was lost in arranging our stands: we were only two guns. I drew the first stand nearer the edge of the forest. Noiselessly, with skis digging deep into the snow, we followed Afanassi. Cold, clear, not a breath of wind, the frost "hanging" in the air, as the Russian saying goes. No dark fir trees in this forest, not like in our northern ones, and everything dazzling white with here and there a patch of rusty brown – a stubborn dead leaf hanging on to an oak tree. I had reckoned with this whiteness and had worn a white shooting suit with several pullovers underneath, but I felt now that the grey fur-lined coat would have been only too welcome. However, white would not show up to the wolves, who are very cautious and have sharp eyes.

I stand now against a birch, sparse brushwood all round me, a few large trees, clusters of yellow reed-like grass here and there. To my right the other gun, my husband, I can't see him but know exactly the direction. To my left, in one or two places, glaring bits of red – the line of red rags drawn along the flank of the beat. Perfect silence reigns everywhere, a silence full of sunshine, of glittering specks and of deep blue shadows. I begin to feel the cold creeping through my clothes: impossible to hold the gun, to touch the steel barrels: my thick knitted gloves feel as if they were made of cobweb, they stick to the steel, and my fingers ache and feel stiff. There, the beaters shout now, from the right to the left the noise grows, now the entire back wall of the beat advances slowly. And my hands ache and are numb. In despair I hang the gun over my arm and dig both hands deep into the slanting side pockets of my coat, trying to move my fingers there so as to bring life to them somehow. My breath freezes into hoarfrost on my eyelashes and eyebrows. I bury my chin into the soft white scarf-like *bashlyk* twisted round my throat and twitch my face to prevent my cheeks from freezing. But I dare not move; to stand still is the first rule the huntsman learns, for the game has sharper eyes than man and it may be watching you from behind some bush long before you ever suspect its presence.

And then suddenly, right in front of me, as if rising out of the snow, appears a wolf, a large and beautiful animal. He stops and looks round, listens to the approaching shouts of the beaters, evidently considering which way to turn to evade them. It is too far to shoot and he stands facing me – the worst possible shot if I wanted to risk it. My hands are still in my pockets, I cannot pull them out now while the wolf is there and watching me and the surroundings. Finally, he makes up his mind and steps in high and light bounds, his proud head well up, his ears moving slightly. He comes straight up to me: thirty paces, I count in my mind, twenty-six paces now separate us. He evidently does not see me, I dare not look at him directly for fear that our eyes meet and he recognises my human eyes – and the danger. Twenty-five paces – I must take out my hands; he turns his head slightly to the right and with a rapid movement I pull my hands out of my pockets, raise the gun and shoot for the neck. It is a heavy gun and knocks me nearly over, I stumble, and when I look up I see the white forest, the blue shadows long and deep, hear the excited shouts of the beaters – and find no trace of the wolf.

Have I missed him? But then I would have seen him go – and I am positive I did not see him go. Where is he? Has he vanished? Petrified, I dare not move, so I wait. The beaters are there, only a few paces away, my husband comes up rapidly on skis, Afanassi runs from the flank wiping the sweat off his brow (lucky him, I think, to be hot in these conditions!) Where is the wolf? Who shot? Where did he go? I don't know what happened – is my only answer. I shot him there, right there, some twenty-three paces from me. And then suddenly shouts of joy – there he is lying in the soft snow, on the very spot I shot at him, buried deep from his own weight. It was a happy moment, but I only begged to get back quickly to the sledges, to let me slip into the fur coat waiting there, to let me run on the skis – only to get warm at last!

Later, at home, sitting in front of the fire, I could relive the excitement of the day and enjoy thoroughly this "classical" beauty of the day's sport. The other wolves had broken through the back line between two beaters who had got stuck in the snow. But judging from the footprints mine was the largest, Afanassi said, and I well believed him, for the proud look and the powerful movements of the animal gave him the air of the "king of the forest".

8

SMALL GAME AND OTHER STORIES FROM LOUISINO

Great Bustards in the Steppes

There is an interesting sport which, I believe, is little known in Europe outside the steppes of southern Russia. It is the shooting of the great bustards in summer or early autumn, when they feed on the harvested fields. This bird, looking rather like a goose on much longer legs, has a dignified, sometimes extremely swift walk, and is very difficult to approach, the more so as it usually keeps to open spaces. The northern part of the steppes, the so-called "black-earth" country, offered plenty of space and food. Fields stretched out as far as the eye could see, unbroken by hedges or trees. It was the granary of Russia with its rich dark earth requiring no deep ploughing, hiding no stones, void of fences, gates, ditches. This country suits the bustard – but gives the stalker little chance of any sort of cover.

I have never come across single bustards, they seem to keep always in groups, close together, and I remember seeing up to twelve, sometimes fifteen birds at a time. They really look magnificent as they walk leisurely on the green autumn-sown wheat or on the freshly ploughed black-earth fields. Their plumage looks nearly white in spite of being well shaded with light-grey and brown, and the movement of their long necks is well timed with their demure strides. In a very nonchalant way they bend to peck right and left and show great alertness when they suddenly stretch out their necks spying danger.

This is how I saw them lying flat on the ground in a field of stubble – the extravagantly high stubble of the village fields in these parts of Russia, where during the harvest, which was done by hand and with the sickle, it was less tiring to cut high without much bending. My gun, ready for use, lay on my left hand; my elbows were getting numb, my shoulder blades felt the strain as they rose high above my head. But I dared not move following intently through the screen of stubble the group of white birds advancing slowly towards me, and beyond them the monotonous, regular movement of a rider. He rode step, his horse hanging its head down quite low – evidently on a very lose bridle – both the rider and the mount looked like a wound up toy as they passed along the horizon line from left to right, from right to left again.

I was fascinated by this movement, by the precise and accurate way in which the rider, when turning his horse back, wielded it round so that it never faced the birds and then resumed his slow progress slanting off his line of advance and thus forcing the birds unnoticeably to move in my – or rather in our – direction.

In fact, some 80 yards or more to my right and as much to my left lay hidden in the stubble my husband and a brother of the rider – certainly watching as intently as I did every movement of the birds. The sun was hot, the air trembled over the surface of the fields, a large green beetle was scrambling up a stalk – so near my eyes that it looked as big as the birds. And the rider, like a ploughman, continued slowly his monotonous movement – coming nearer and nearer – a sight to which the birds must be well accustomed and of which they are not frightened.

Slowly they approach our line a little closer to the left wing – nearer my husband. I could visualise him, lying in the stubble like myself, his gun ready, his finger on the trigger, perhaps pushing impatiently into place with a quick movement his dark-rimmed shooting spectacles. The beetle in front of me was now level with my eyes, huge and so awkward as it climbed with difficulty up the smooth stalk of wheat – towards such a disillusion, I thought, as there was nothing on the top.

And then suddenly a distant neighing on my right – it must be one of our horses getting impatient – if only the groom could manage to keep them quiet! The light four-seater brake had brought us here about an hour ago, when we first sighted the birds from a considerable distance. Having decided to try our luck we had left the road and had driven slowly across the stubble several hundred yards from the birds, leaving them on our right. Then, one by one, we dropped or rather rolled off the brake on the side where the birds could not see us fall. It was a kind of dive one had to take hugging the gun with one arm and stretching out the other to soften the fall. First my husband rolled out – more complicated for him as he had his shotgun and a Winchester rifle; then came my turn and I plunged head forward into the stubble keeping the muzzle of my gun high so as not to get it full of earth. The order had been then to lie motionless and to wait. Everything seemed to have worked well – if only the horses there in the back would keep quiet. But no! They neigh again – the birds stop abruptly and look around. What bad luck! A few more yards and my husband could have shot relying upon the excellent range of his 12-bore. Holding my breath I waited – the rider seemed imperturbable and I only hoped that his horse would keep quiet and would not be tempted to answer his stable companions. And then suddenly the screeching of wheels in bad need of greasing – somewhere behind us. I peep cautiously over my shoulder: in the direction of the high road a long trail of dust is rising and my ear catches the wild strains of the "Kamarinskaia" – the celebrated dancing song born in these steppes and known all over Russia. Loud and slow at first, it grows faster and faster, louder and louder, out of rhythm though, tottering, whirling, shouted lustily by a strong young voice – a bit husky. Evidently someone returning from town after a successful deal celebrated at the "tractir" [the pub]. "The fool! The idiot!" I think, scarcely daring to look at our birds. How lovely they look now as they stretch out their long necks, spread their wings, take a few running steps and rise above the ground. A beautiful take off – and a dry, short crack of a rifle – on my left – one of the birds sways, seems to leap up – and falls clumsily to the ground. The others are in full flight and it is a lovely sight, I can't look at the white bundle lying now motionless in the stubble. The rider waves his hand but he too is obviously following with his eyes the lovely sight of the birds in

Letter dated 30 January 1918 from the Lissino District Rural Committee informing "citizeness Eedita Feodorovna Sologub" of a meeting to dispose of her estate according to the laws of the Russian Republic. She resolved to attend this meeting despite the possible dangers (see p. 151).

Coachman Ivan at Waldensee, with carriage and newly planted avenue of trees. 1898.

The children's pony Mousy harnessed to a sledge for Vladimir and Alec. Kamenka 1914.

Vladimir leading Mousy with Alec astride the pony's back. Kamenka 1914.

Hunting wolves with borzois, on the edge of the steppe. An event seldom photographed. This is the moment of calm before the first sighting of a wolf in the distance.

Summer scene in the north, with silver birch and hay barn. Photograph taken by Edith's son Vladimir with his first camera.

Edith relaxing with her gun in a forest glade. This was on one of her last "poaching" escapades in the forests near her former home.

Photograph of Edith with her first bear. Her husband was proud of her achievement, but she felt somewhat tired and bewildered. This photograph found its way in 1912 into the pages of *The Illustrated London News*, in an issue featuring life in Russia.

Edith's prowess with the gun was demonstrated in a 1915 bear hunt attended by the Japanese Ambassador in the imperial forest near Kamenka. The other men in the photograph were imperial forestry employees.

Edith's husband Sasha (second from left) with friends and a wolf he had shot in the forest. It was customary after a day's shooting to pose for the camera. This photograph also featured in *The Illustrated London News* in 1912.

flight, now increasing their speed. The happy song goes on, loud and stumbling, husky and sonorous.

My husband hurries towards the bird calling out to me, "That idiot would have spoilt the day if I had not had my rifle!"

True, there would have been no bag – but certainly it would not have meant for me a "spoilt day", for the excitement of the suspense and the sight of the great birds in flight would always remain a vivid picture among my sporting recollections.

Snipe Shooting in Kursk

"Do we go to the Pochepskia *Luzhi* (pools) or to Assozkoe *Boloto* (swamp)?" I hear myself asking my husband hesitatingly, hoping that he will decide for the first, my favourite place to start the day on snipe. Both places were our regular shooting grounds when the snipe season opened on 15 July. In fact we always came to our Kursk estate in time for this shooting and every time I asked myself – shall I make it? Am I worse than last year? Shall I be quick enough? All very troublesome questions when you are very young and when you have a husband who is first of all an excellent shot and secondly a man who hates women to interfere with any manly sports. To live up to his high standard was not an easy task and at the time gave me quite a bit of worry.

"I prefer to start with the Pochepskia today," answers my husband. "It is early and we have time to get through them by noon. The Assozkoe can do for the afternoon."

All right – this arrangement suits me perfectly, for the *luzhi* seem friendly to me and to miss a snipe there is less of a shame than to miss one on the wide open space of Assozkoe. In fact, the *luzhi* were an ideal place for any water fowl or moor bird and it had the charm of offering always some unexpected surprises – so my husband had told me before I had ever been there and I experienced it myself in later years.

We were on the steps of the front door. The coachman was holding the pair of greys harnessed to the shooting brake of local production – a sort of wickerwork body reminding me of a large laundry basket, supplied with two seats and resting on long wooden poles fixed to the axles; an extremely light carriage, soft to drive in, and very handy for use on bad roads. We drove it in turns. Both dogs, Sport and Fingo, were already on the front seat; Sport trembling like a nervous actor before appearing on the stage, Fingo looking glum — because he could not smile, I suppose. Both were obviously very eager to go.

It was early, about five in the morning, and the air was still relatively cool. Even the dust seemed reluctant to rise as we turned from the long drive into the big road — and it really was big even though it scarcely deserved the title of road. It was the old *shliakh*, one of the main arterial roads built by the Empress Catherine II in the second half of the eighteenth century to link the wild South with Moscow. Road engineering was certainly at a primitive stage then — in Russia at least — but there was no meanness in conception: this *shliakh* ran as straight as a Roman road for miles, was bordered in parts by huge old birches and was some 70 yards wide. It was in fact nothing more than a beaten track with no engineering art ever applied to it, and the traffic ran where it suited the drivers at any given moment, or where the peasant horses chose to go when the caravans of carts made their way to town or to the sugar factory with the peasants sleeping peacefully on their goods, the front horse alone carrying all responsibility for the long file behind it.

We jerked into the ruts of the moment and drove in silence straight south, leaving the dried up pond and the village on our left. The park on the banks of this so-called pond looked mysterious and gloomy in the dull light of a summer morning. The fields all around us were wrapped in a light haze of dust — inches deep and rising behind us like a cloud.

"It will be hot today," said my husband. "We'll do the *luzhi* quickly to put the horses in the oak grove of Assozkoe by noon. How many cartridges did you take?"

"I think 50 of the small shot — 8 — and 25 of the rougher in case we come across some duck later in the day."

"That should do. Don't forget to wait for the proper moment to shoot your snipe — if you miss you'll ruin your dog, you know."

Yes, I knew it well enough and trembled in anticipation.

The *luzhi* were there — the strangest marsh I ever saw — some 15 acres of boggy land lost among the fields in the heart of the steppes! How the water came there and why it ever stayed there was a mystery to me. There was no apparent declivity, no sign of former brooks or rivers anywhere near. Just green, swampy grass, reeds and rushes surrounding a number of larger and smaller ponds with dark boggy water; no connection between these ponds' high tufts of dry grass sticking on lumps of turf. The snipe preferred the green swampy stretches and sometimes could be found there in great numbers – later in the season especially when the migrating crowds stopped in this place for the usual rests. There were, however, also local snipe – those that bred in the place, and we really counted upon these for the start.

Both dogs were away before my husband had tied up the horses. I followed the couple with my 20-bore, hoping that nothing would rise before my husband took his dog, Sport. Sport was quicker than my Fingo, and had a very good nose. Fingo followed him, looking more conscientiously into details; he had a great respect and blind faith in Sport's efficiency and whenever Sport pointed Fingo would follow his example – fortunately for a second or two only, withdrawing most carefully to pursue his own task.

Sport stopped dead on my right, Fingo flattened himself in the grass; my heart beat much too fast. There – a cautious encouragement from my husband behind me – to Sport to push on (not to me) – and the graceful silhouette of the snipe rises against the brilliant eastern sky. I hesitate – it is so lovely – and is it the right second? "Shoot!" – I do – and I miss! Sports lifts his head and looks after the bird in flight – then at me with a reproachful look.

"Why did you wait? Of course you'll miss if you try to shoot after the twist. Don't be too quick with the next though – that won't do either!" was all the comment I got, and we separated so as to cover more rapidly the space of clear, green swamp. Another shot a few minutes later and Sport was picking up the snipe. Poor Fingo looked offended – I had not given him any satisfaction yet. Still – his turn came too and we each had our chances and good results before we approached the real ponds.

The sun was high now, it was getting hot and it was heavy walking in the slushy, soft ground. My husband had just told

LOUISINO: SMALL GAME AND OTHER STORIES

me to tie my handkerchief round my cap as he could not see me otherwise in the high reeds and grass. We had not gone far asunder yet when I noticed Sport's motionless figure in the grass and a second later my husband shot the rising snipe – and then, turning swiftly to the right, fired his second barrel. I could see no bird falling, none flying, except a couple of duck in the distance. "What was it?" I called out as I saw my husband dashing into the rushes, paying no attention to Sport with his snipe.

"A fox" he called back. "Come to help find him if he is only wounded!"

I rushed to the spot followed by Fingo, with poor Sport standing still over his bird. My husband was already holding up the fox, a lean, light yellow animal, as they are in those parts of the country.

"That was a fine right and left – and with snipe shot, too! Congratulations!" I said. "But how on earth could a fox be here, in the swamp?

"He was doing his bit of hunting, stalking the duck that flew up from this puddle after my first shot," said my husband. "I could just see something yellow disappearing behind that lump of grassy turf, and got it as it dashed round the other." He was obviously pleased and amused at this unusual right and left, and turned round to whistle for Sport. There he was, wagging his tail with a smile on his faithful face, the snipe at his feet. But he showed no interest whatever in the fox, and probably blamed his master for wasting time on such unusual game.

This is but one of the unusual right and left shots my husband made on the *luzhi* – twice again in later days he had an uncommon couple: once a snipe and a large white owl, another time a duck and a hare.

A Badger Hunt

It all happened many years ago. We were spending the autumn months in Louisino and time flew as we were free to hunt and to ride as much as we liked, and my husband's duties with the local self-government were light at this time of year. It happened though once that he was called away to some urgent meeting and

125

I found myself rather at a loss, being unwilling to go out shooting alone because of the big distances. As I was coming home from a short ride across the fields stretching out into the steppe a peasant boy brought me a short note from our old uncle who had an estate a few miles away.

"Come over, Edith dear, you might find it amusing to go badger hunting with me. I'll wait until three," said the note.

I was delighted, and having warned my mother-in-law I rode off without delay. It was more pleasant to ride across the fields than to drive in the dogcart through the long and dusty village with crowds of urchins gaping and shouting. Just before three I was at the gate of Uncle Levan's place, such a delightfully cosy little place with its orchards and flower gardens, its low white house and rows of sunflowers which seemed to prosper there better than anywhere else. It all looked so gay and friendly in the bright sunshine and so did my old uncle with his flowing white beard and red face as he stood on the terrace steps welcoming me.

"Don't get off your horse, I'll join you right away," he called out just as Aunt Ata appeared in the doorstep smiling and looking a little anxious and worried as she always did. They had married late in life and neither had ever got over their "bachelor" and "spinster" ways, especially Aunt Ata, who always fretted around her sport-loving and lively husband. However, in a couple of minutes we were really off, Uncle Levan riding one of his charming small Arab horses and followed by two rather disreputable looking gamekeepers with a couple of non-descript mongrels.

We soon reached the badger wood stretching over low hills and small valleys with a thick growth of pines, birches and thickets of hazelnut bushes. We left the horses at the bottom of the main valley and slowly walked uphill while the mongrels started "looking busy" but were not in the least efficient, I thought. Uncle Levan knew where the badgers had their burrows and we soon reached the place, which looked to me remarkably dry and bright compared to the badger haunts I knew in Kamenka. At this time of the day and with the warm sunshine we expected the badgers to be in their burrows, and the mongrels were quite certain of it, for they immediately dashed for the first entrance we came to.

Uncle Levan was in his element, giving orders and organising the attack.

"Control the dogs! Dmitri!" he was calling to one of the gamekeepers who was already clutching the tail of one of his mongrels half buried in the burrow. "Watch over the entrances behind the bushes, Peter! And you, Edith, go up to the left and see to the exit there, I'll join you at once."

And so it went on, with the two men interrupting him respectfully.

"You see, Sir, there is a back door," Peter was saying.

"It might be safer . . ." Dmitri put in.

"Don't interrupt me. I know about that door – and hold Sharik, he'll slip in and he is too young to face the old badger by himself. Let the mother in first . . .!"

At last we were all posted, with Ivan, the young gamekeeper who had just joined us, placed near the back door with a hazelnut stick as his only weapon.

"And mind that nothing slips through, Ivan! If you keep good watch and catch the badger you'll get as much vodka as you can get down in one evening!" called out Uncle Levan cheerfully, "And if you don't – you'll remain a fool all your life."

"I'll try my best, Sir," was the reply, and Ivan scampered uphill while our attention was already concentrated on the growls that could be heard now coming from underground.

The moment was tense: the growls and grunts in the burrow, the yelps of the young dog pulling frantically at his leash, the loud whispers of Uncle Levan – and all our attention directed towards the various exits. Suddenly Uncle Levan, who was lying down with his ear to the ground, called out,

"Dmitri! Let loose the other dog – I'll let him in to help his mother, they are having a regular fight down there!"

The young mongrel, roused to the highest pitch of excitement listening to his mother's voice, dashed forward and disappeared in the hole under my uncle's command. A few more minutes of tense anxiety, then a scuffle, growls, muffled barks – and the triumphant voice of Ivan shouting from higher up behind the bushes,

"I've got him – help me to hold him . . . and call off the dogs quick . . . Poshel! Brys!"

A loud whine, angry grunts, more curses from Ivan. We were rushing up the hill, uncle Levan red with excitement, panting away with a whizz,

"Hold on! We are coming! Hold tight!"

We burst out on to the little clearing and here was Ivan crouching on the ground holding with both hands a shapeless, wriggling bundle and kicking frantically with bare legs at the infuriated mongrels.

"What's happened, Ivan? Hold on, let me help you . . ." Uncle Levan was calling now.

"It's all right, Sir! I am holding him tight . . . but I can't get up . . . the Countess. . . . I have no trousers . . .!"

We burst out laughing. There was Ivan crouching as low as he could, his hairy legs warding off the dogs with low side kicks and holding tight his trousers in which the badger was wriggling frantically.

"How on earth did the beast get into your trousers, Ivan? Edith, turn round for a moment until we get the badger out of the trousers and Ivan back into them again – if they are still of any use!" Uncle Levan called out gaily.

I waited for a few moments listening to the laughter of the men, the barking of the dogs. The badger was evidently successfully slipped into a bag and Ivan found his trousers none the worse for the experience.

"Everything all right, Edith! And now tell us, Ivan, how did you manage this trick?" Uncle Levan was saying, still laughing. Ivan was red and beaming, wiping the sweat off his forehead with the back of his hand.

"Well, Sir, you said I was to catch it and I knew the mother badger can bite. What was I to do? So I took my trousers off, tied up both legs with my belt and fastened one side of the trousers firmly to the ground with a stick and held the other with both hands. And right enough, the growls and the fighting got nearer, and then a thud and a rush and I just had time to catch the trousers before they were swept away on the badger's nose! I held fast – and it was not easy!"

"Molodets! [Well done!] – made you a bit thirsty. The vodka will soon put things straight – you know – only don't go too quickly at it, or what will Dunia say? Eh?" laughed Uncle Levan, while Ivan, still smiling all over his face, answered,

"Dunia! It isn't for nothing that she is my wife! She'll scold me for that tear in the trousers anyhow, but she'll be pleased, that I know!"

A Chaotic Fox Hunt

Of course we shot foxes in Russia, firstly because hunting as such is known only in a very restricted part of the country and only among a very limited number of people; secondly, because we had many foxes which had to be exterminated in districts where hunting would otherwise have been impossible. In fact, if you spoke of killing foxes, you always meant shooting them, with dogs or without dogs, depending on the region.

In the Kursk province we were already on the border of the steppes. However, there were also many wooded areas cut by rows of deep gullies, former beds of brooks, their banks covered with a thick growth of hazelnut bushes, young oaks bristling around the old stumps and some birches. In fact these were only the remains of old forests which had been mercilessly cut and devastated and where the young growth had never been trimmed and cared for. It was a heartache for us to see this devastation, but the mischief had been done long before our time and we could not easily remedy it. These gullies, often a system of small valleys running into one, were the favourite haunts of foxes, which could easily dig their lairs in the light, partly sandy soil. The thick undergrowth gave them excellent cover.

Having had many complaints of the havoc done by foxes in a village near a distant farm belonging to us, my husband decided one day to have a good go at these foxes, and two neighbours were asked to join us. Everything was soon organised: we were to spend the night at the house of one of these neighbours, Vsevolod, as his place was near our farm, where we had no accommodation for ourselves. And so, on a clear and cool September morning we set out late, as was always the case when one stayed at Vsevolod's. As the light shooting brakes and simple carts carrying the sportsmen and the local gamekeepers with the dogs stopped at the edge of a small wood, I was puzzled to see four or five totally unknown individuals carrying guns and obviously joining our party. Having asked my husband about these people I found that he too was at a loss and had to ask Vsevolod for an explanation.

"Oh, they are my coachman, my foreman and my chef – they like shooting. They are very bad shots – but why not let them have their bit of fun?" answered Vsevolod with his usual bonhomie.

"All right," said my husband good-naturedly, but I felt a note of doubt in his voice.

It was decided first to comb through several fields where groups of bushes had formed islands and where the foxes were known to lie in wait for hares. The dogs very soon picked up the scent of game – whether they were foxes or hares could not be distinguished, as the dogs were as untrained as the local gamekeepers. Anyhow, they were on the trail of something, and we, the guns, advancing in a row, soon had the opportunity of shooting. The first shots were at hares and my husband took several of them in a short time, all the other guns missing cheerfully with a lot of noise, with numbers of double shots, much shouting and running after hares supposed to have been hit. This rather startled me as the absolute disorder of the line made it difficult to shoot. We now approached the main system of gullies where the dogs had disappeared apparently on the hot scent of a fox.

"You'll stay with me," said my husband. "With these men armed and unable to shoot properly one never knows."

"Very well – we'll shoot and shout together, if necessary," I said jokingly. But little did I realise how very close to the truth I was when speaking about shouting too.

The sun was hot by now and the gully a real splendour of golden and brown leaves with patches of pale and yellow grass at the bottom. It was one of those clear transparent autumn days when the air is light and not yet hard with the cold winds. We crossed the main valley together and presently separated from the rest of the guns, at any rate from Vsevolod and his cousin. The chef, coachman and others who had cropped up from somewhere had disappeared right at the start. The dogs could be heard in the valley now but no one seemed really interested in them. However, there was a whole chorus working well together, obviously following the same scent, and we got our guns ready.

"You go to the right," said my husband to Vsevolod, "along the main valley and keep an eye on that. We'll follow the valley bearing off towards the left, keeping near the top. So don't worry and shoot along the bottom and halfway up, we'll be near the upper edge."

Vsevolod gave a big laugh. "How pedantic you are! We run where we think best and shoot wherever nothing seems to be in the way, it's all very simple!"

"I don't agree with this system, but I suppose it may work all right. I'll keep to mine. So, au revoir, for the present."

Vsevolod waved his hand and walked off, waddling along the bottom of the main valley. We climbed up the side of the offshoot gully and had just reached the top of it when the dogs gave a frantic burst, apparently making towards us halfway up the slope.

"Keep an eye on these bushes there," said my husband, cocking his gun. I was ready with mine.

Something reddish-yellow flashed among the hazel bushes – a fox, right across the gully. A shot from my husband and the fox comes down bumping against the trunks and rolling towards the bottom of the gully. At the same moment two men come dashing down the hillock shooting lustily at the rolling fox.

"Damn them! Out of the way or I'll shoot," shouted my husband with a stentorian roar, "Don't you see the fox is dead? You fools!"

The two men whom I now recognised to be the chef and the foreman stopped short and, wiping their foreheads with the back of their hands, said somewhat apologetically,

"We thought the fox was still running. Sorry, Sir."

"You thought! Don't think but keep your eyes open and look out next time before you shoot," said my husband, who was now approaching the fox and trying to get the dogs off it. "Call your dogs away!" he called out as they were tearing fiercely at the fox.

"Sorry, Sir. They never obey anyone, except perhaps the gamekeeper Timoshka," answered one of the men.

"Well then, get Timoshka, and quickly too!" shouted my husband, trying in vain to rescue the fox before it was torn to shreds.

Shouts of "Timoshka, here! Timoshka, here!" rent the gully and a bearded man scampered down the slope, gun in hand, stumbling over roots and stumps. As he reached us I noticed that the old shotgun he carried at a level had both triggers cocked. Noticing it too, my husband called out to him.

"Let down the triggers first – and then tackle your dog!"

Timoshka looked at us stupidly, then down at his gun with a puzzled expression, then let down the triggers leisurely and dashed for the dogs with a volley of oaths. Apparently this was the right thing to do and the dogs let go the fox, half torn by now. As we turned round we saw Vsevolod coming down in haste, red and sweaty and beaming as usual.

"Have you got one?" he shouted.

"Yes, an old one," answered my husband, "And look here, Vsevolod, you had better keep the triggers of your gun down too when you rush through the thicket."

"Oh, do you think so? – Well, it may be better, you are right. You see when my brother was killed by his groom last year it just happened that there was an unfortunate branch in the way of the groom as the latter scampered down a slope, and the gun went off and killed my brother – real bad luck . . . but fate, after all," said Vsevolod, making the sign of the cross.

"Maybe it was fate and maybe just a stupid accident," said my husband. "And I don't want to give a stupid accident the opportunity of trying itself out on me, or on my wife."

Vsevolod laughed, "Of course not, I understand. Such accidents don't happen so often, after all. This one happened last year, so we need not expect one this year, don't you think so?"

"Well, I don't know the habit of accidents in general and prefer not to investigate. Can your man take this fox to the carriage, please?"

Vsevolod gave the order to one of his men and we continued our shoot. The dogs were already on another scent and were now in full swing on it. We took up our positions behind a cluster of large hazel bushes and waited for the approaching pack. A few moments later I saw a fox slinking through the bushes and shot at it. Nothing happened, I wondered where the fox had vanished.

"Good shot! He's down on the spot," said my husband, and barely had we left our bush to pick up the fox before the dogs could set on it when a volley of shots coming from across the valley riddled our bushes. This time my husband really did shout at the men whose red and blank faces appeared now through the thicket.

"Please, excuse us, Sir, we did not know you were near," said the coachman, accompanied by the groom. "We just saw the fox . . ."

"Look out for live foxes before you shoot and first make sure where you shoot," were my husband's only comments.

And so it went on all day: dogs giving tongue in all directions, three foxes killed and twelve seen, volleys of shots interspersed with oaths, men running up and down the gully wiping the sweat off their faces and dragging their guns with lifted triggers.

As we were driving home in the glorious sunset of a hot September day my husband turned to Vsevolod,

"It has been a good day and it is nice to be able to say so with an easy heart after seeing all your men rushing round like madmen trailing their guns and shooting right and left. I did not think we'd all survive!"

"Oh, that's nothing!" said Vsevolod gaily. Accidents need not happen and I generally shout when I am behind a bush and wave my white cap too, as a warning."

"The foxes must be thankful too," said my husband.

"Well, well, you chaps from up north have too many ideas about organised shoots, too many complications for us here," retorted Vsevolod, who never missed an opportunity of pointing out the difference between the northerners and the southern folk from the steppe.

"Perhaps I prefer, though, the idea of shooting a fox rather than shooting your chef, which would leave us without the good dinner we were looking forward to," replied my husband. But as we all joked about it Vsevolod had to agree that a certain degree of safety is quite pleasant after all – even for a "southerner".

The Homing Instinct of Horses

One often reads about the homing instinct of horses, but one rarely has the opportunity, here in Western Europe, to put one's own horses to the test. Quite by chance I have twice had experiences which struck me as evident proof of the horses' instinct, and both times with horses bred on our estate.

Both incidents occurred in Central Russia shortly before the First World War, when we were spending part of the winter in Louisino. It was a severe winter and masses of snow covered the boundless stretch of steppes. Fortunately, the high road to the railway station and the little market town some twelve miles away was well marked by huge old birches, which had once bordered the road on either side but which then were already sparse. To begin with the old birches were replaced, but this had no longer been done regularly, since the railway had reduced the importance of the road. However, the birches could be seen here and there and that was enough even when the road was entirely covered by snowdrifts several feet deep. This was, in fact, the only road we used in winter.

One day, however, we had to go to friends who had only recently settled in the neighbourhood and whose place was some ten miles away, but not on the high road. Our coachman said that he knew the way and we reached the house in good time for an early dinner; we were there at about five o'clock. We had driven through a sea of white fields with the sleigh tracks at many points covered by snowdrifts and marked with branches stuck in the snow, but only on the approaches to our own and to the other village – for a couple of hundred yards at most. Snow had again begun to fall when we reached our destination, but neither my husband nor I paid much attention to it.

Our hosts were young and cheerful, the old house delightful with heavy mahogany furniture and incredible portraits of ancestors, all painted by serf artists a century or so ago. The dinner was an amusing disharmony of really good old Russian provincial cooking and limp attempts at French cuisine. We stayed until about nine, but then insisted on leaving, as we counted upon the moon which, though decreasing, should have been helpful.

We started all right through the village, found the marking branches on leaving it and continued slowly through the thick falling snow. It felt as if we were swimming through thick white foam. My husband asked the coachman whether he was sure of the way. "Yes," was the answer, and the moon shone faintly on the endless white surface.

We drove very slowly, but after about an hour the coachman began to jump off his seat, trying to find the road underfoot while the three horses stood panting and snorting after their heavy work. My husband and the coachman discussed the probabilities and possibilities of our being on the road or not, but it was evident that we were off the track and neither of the two had any idea where to go, as even to retrace our steps would have been difficult through the curtain of falling snow and in the very faint moonlight. The prospect of spending the night in the open sledge was not attractive, since even fur coats do not give adequate protection against the bitterly cold wind sweeping over the steppe.

Finally my husband ordered the coachman to let the horses find their own way. We set off slowly; though snorting loudly and panting hard the horses did not seem to hesitate and stopped only once or twice to take breath. By midnight we saw in front of us the slowly rising dark row of poplars that bordered our apple orchards. The horses had taken us straight home, not along the road, which lay a good way to the left, but straight as the crow flies. What amused me was that once the row of poplars was reached the horses seemed to hesitate which way to turn. Obviously they had never approached the orchards from this side and probably felt here the need of a guiding hand.

I may mention that the two flank horses of our troika were young and had been broken in early that winter: they had been driven only along the high road. The horse in the shafts was an older one, and probably he had been the leader.

* * *

The other incident left an even more vivid impression upon me as that time I was the driver. It took place at the beginning of

October in the same estate in Kursk. My husband, my brother and I had been shooting all day on an extensive bog some ten miles from home. We had left our horses at the house of a friend on a height above this lowland. After an excellent day's shooting we returned tired and famished to this friend's house where we were expected to stay for dinner. She was a kind old lady, pressingly hospitable, and it was difficult to get away. We had a riding horse on which I had come in the morning and a small light shooting-brake with a pair of young greys. As we got out on the steps of the veranda we realised how pitch dark it was and my husband willingly accepted the offer of a stable lantern to take with us. He mounted my horse and rode in front, lighting the way for us. As my brother disliked horses in general and young ones in particular, I took the reins while he held the guns so that they should not be damaged by the bumpiness of the road.

We reached the fields past the backs of the village houses successfully and turned east – homewards. I must note here that country roads in those parts were frequently nothing more than a track – two ruts in the soft black earth, cutting through the fields which belonged to large village communities. These fields were divided into narrow strips according to the number of families of the particular village. When ploughing these strips the peasants did not bother to lift their ploughs where the road cut across their strip, with the result that the tracks suddenly disappeared into ploughland. Obviously this complicated matters considerably as the road we had managed to trace in the morning had been ploughed over in the course of the day.

My husband rode from side to side ahead of us, trying to trace the constantly vanishing track and giving me orders: "Go right," "Don't follow me," "Stop and wait," and so on. The horses became nervous, as they were young and not used to night drives; my brother cursed the bumping on the ploughed land; the dogs at our feet whined discreetly as we hopped across the furrows. To drive was particularly tiring, as the horses tugged at the reins – and with the Russian harness one has four heavy woven reins in the hand for a pair of horses. Finally, my husband called out, "I can't find anything! Let the horses find their way – they'll scent home. Mine can't as it's a new one."

I held the reins, but did not attempt to guide. The horses began their usual spacious trot (they were cross-bred Orloff trotters out of half-Percheron mares). I had only to hold them back to spare my poor brother a little. "They are going well," called out my husband, "They'll make it!"

"If our bones stick it," murmured my brother.

"Yes, and as long as they get us over the bridge!" I added.

"What? The rickety bridge?" said my brother, anxiously. "You'll never make it – I'll get out when we are there!"

At this moment the lantern carried by my husband went out and we were hopelessly in the dark and going at a good pace.

* * *

How long we went I do not know, but suddenly the sound under the hoofs and the wheels was different, softer, grassy. I knew it must be the green strip above the bridge, and before I had time to warn my brother the horses plunged left pulling the brake down the slanting slope that led to the bridge. I held the reins tight and hoped for the best.

This bridge, spanning a narrow gully with steep banks, was just wide enough for two horses abreast, had no railings and was made of rows of thin trunks loosely put across three beams. It was a primitive construction and dangerous even in daylight – but then, in that darkness! The horses clattered with their hoofs, they both hit the bridge, and we thundered across with my husband following us closely, relying on the clatter for direction. My brother gasped when we were halfway across: "The bridge! And you never told me!"

We galloped up the opposite bank, then came a sharp corner to the left, and the front wheel caught it too high. "Lean left! Hold tight!" I called out, not daring to pull right because of the steep bank there. We seemed to hang for a second on the right wheels, then banged back on all four and reached the road safely. Fortunately there were no banks, no hedges, no ditches along this high road and a few yards farther we reached the stone columns – the old gateway and the drive to our house.

Only on handing the reins to the coachman who was waiting at the door and on getting out of the brake did I realise how absolutely stiff I was – and how tired! It had been a strain and, I knew, a very close shave. But here again the young horses, left to their instinct, had found their way home, and they had not been more than once before to the place we came from. But they did know the bridge – we had used this crossing several times. Still, how they got the right direction across those ploughed fields and how they took the slanting descent is a marvel to me.

Kazim the Amorous Georgian

Our pack of borzois was giving us a lot of trouble. They were lovely dogs, given us by the Grand Duke Nicolas from his celebrated kennels of Pershino, and by now we had twelve of them. Long silky coats, wiry curved backs and snake-like narrow heads with large, attentive eyes. They needed a good deal of exercise and we simply could not find a suitable man who could be trusted with them.

My husband and I used to take them out daily for a quick gallop in the evening but this meant coming home early from shooting snipe and quail, which we liked to do for entire days. Besides, we did not feel quite fit for a gallop after hard walking from dawn to dusk over swamps and fields of stubble. We tried to remedy the situation by letting the borzois out into a large courtyard, but invariably they managed to spy a cat, or a hen or a turkey in some remote corner and a passionate but very short chase ensued, followed by sour remarks from my mother-in-law, who owned the estate. Obviously something had to be done as we could not send the dogs to our own place in the wooded northern areas where there were no open spaces for hunting with borzois.

And then one day the beautiful Kazim turned up, an apparition of outlandish splendour in these central-Russian steppes. He was a Georgian, a true Caucasian, there could be no doubt about it as he sauntered up to the terrace, narrow face, black eyes, broad shoulders and a wasp's waist. But, above all, his clothes were the most striking, both in shape and in colour: the well-tailored blue cloth coat with cartridge pockets on the chest, with a narrow

138

silver belt and a high black fur cap (in August, when we were dying with heat!).

We found out that he was looking for a job but as he could give no references at all and could not even explain his presence here, in the Kursk province, thousands or more miles from the Caucasus, my husband refused to take him, and the beautiful apparition had to leave. However, the next morning he was on the farm again, this time in a soft nasturtia-coloured coat, his high boots with pointed toes shining in the sunshine.

"I wonder where that fellow spent the night," said my husband, "He could not get out to town and be back here so early again."

"I forgot to tell you. I had my suspicions last night that he never left when you sent him away, for when I went round the garden with the dog I heard a lot of laughing and joking near the stables and a strange man's voice with a foreign accent among the lot!" I said.

My husband laughed. "That's it, the girls have already fallen for him, and no wonder with his brilliant outfit. I fear we'll have to take him, otherwise he'll be sneaking round the place without Mother's authorisation – and that would be worse."

Thus Kazim was interviewed again: he was made to ride one of the young horses for a test and showed undoubtedly a good seat and a firm hand, although he seemed to be little used to the so-called English saddle. Then he was sent to our uncle, a dear old gentleman whose estate was some five miles away and who was a Caucasian prince himself. My husband and I drove there in the afternoon and after due injunctions (in an incomprehensible language) on the part of the uncle, Kazim promised to obey our orders, to look after the borzois and to take care of the two horses entrusted to him for exercising the dogs. At last we seemed to have a solution to our problem and could breathe a sigh of relief.

That same night, as we were having supper, unusual noises, shrieks and furious barking of dogs drew our attention. My husband went out onto the terrace and immediately called us hurriedly to join him. Indeed the picture was worth seeing, and listening to: the large courtyard of the farm was bathed in the silvery light of the full moon, clouds of dust rose from the centre of the yard and a number of figures were clustering along the walls of the farm buildings. It was Kazim, who was giving a perfect display of the Caucasian riding tricks: his coat – it was white this time – was swinging round him and the red *bashlyk* (a special kind of cloth hood with long ends serving as a scarf) thrown over his shoulders whirled like the wings of some strange night bird as he twisted his horse in all directions, made it rear and sit back on its haunches, thrusting it suddenly into a wild gallop round the well and the watering troughs, then disappearing suddenly from the saddle but still clinging to it in some mysterious way. It was a fantastic display in this silvery light of the moon, the clouds of fine black-earth dust billowing in the overhanging shade of centenarian limes framing in the yard from two sides. We were simply fascinated, and the shrieks of the girls as Kazim dashed with loose reins into their midst were certainly full of admiration, not so much of terror. But the men were silent as they stood in a separate group near the stables.

"Well, Mother, I fear you'll have no end of trouble with the girls now. My advice is you keep the younger ones on the other farm. The older matrons can face here, both the work and Kazim!" said my husband as we were stepping back into the house.

"You may be right, my dear, but with the horses you let Kazim have he will surely be on the other farm soon enough, especially in the evenings," and my mother-in-law shook her head thoughtfully.

From then on, when we returned in the evening from shooting, Kazim would meet us on horseback with no borzois and always with a new gaily coloured coat.

"Where are you off to, Kazim," my husband asked every time.

"Off into the stubbles to give this horse some exercise; I used the other one in the morning with the borzois," was Kazim's invariable reply.

And at home we heard more and more complaints that Kazim had not exercised the borzois, that everyone had hunted high and low for him until he had eventually been found sound asleep in some hay loft or barn. And then the men began to grumble and to murmur, and it was not long before their complaints came in droves: Ivan's wife was not working anymore, forgetting to prepare supper. Peter's wife insisted on being sent to the other farm where the girls were, Dmitri's neglected her children and spent the day at her window watching the drive along which Kazim used to take the borzois out – if and when he did so – my poor mother-in-law was in distress with this shower of complaints and finally gave us an ultimatum: both Kazim and the borzois must go unless we could find a more suitable man. The old lady was right, of course, so after a family council it was decided to appeal to the kind uncle who would know how to deal with Kazim, who was duly sent to him. He departed wearing his white cloth Sunday coat, with his tall black cap well pushed back. His horse pranced and stepped like a circus horse, the matrons gaped from all the windows, the men muttered oaths and turned their backs.

I don't know what the uncle said, but we were told that Kazim returned only at dawn, bundled his collection of clothes and departed unnoticed on the nice grey horse and without waiting for his salary. That day the farm was in a flutter: the matrons were on strike and cried their eyes out, the men used freely very strong language and applied energetic measures to bring their womenfolk back into line, and the girls from the other farm, we were told later, went en masse to the crossroads to see Kazim pass and take tearful leave of him. For months the word Kazim had an electrifying effect on the whole farm population; joy in some eyes, taciturn suspicion in others, delighted shrieks from the children – but no one remained passive. That first evening display in the moonlight had brought new impressions of colour, skill and dashing strength which had struck the imagination of the dullest among the onlookers and awakened new ideals of manly beauty in the women's hearts.

LAKE LADOGA
AND THE GULF
OF FINLAND

9

WATERFOWL AND OTHER STORIES FROM LAKE LADOGA AND THE GULF OF FINLAND

Lake Ladoga I: Crossing

Strangely enough, we inhabitants of St. Petersburg, born and bred there, knew very little about the Ladoga Lake outside what one learnt in one's geography lesson. Perhaps it was due to the fact that it was a "serious" lake – that is, a stormy and fitful expanse of water – and that in winter it was partly frozen and so stormy that there was no fun in going there, and in summer we all went to our country places and only very few of them were near the lake. In fact, I began to hear more about it only when I grew up and came across men interested in shooting. Their tales of the variety of game on the lake, of the huge stretches of lowlands covered with reeds forming its southern and partly eastern shores, of the large rivers flowing into it and of the tiny fishing villages inhabited only in summer and erected on tall beams stuck into the water with huts built on wooden floors and interconnected by plank bridges – all this fascinated me and sharpened my curiosity. But it was only in 1917–19, since the outbreak of the revolution, that I succeeded in going to Lake Ladoga, first because of the fishing there and later for shooting.

My interest in the fishing was purely commercial at first: the masses of fish brought in daily from part of the eastern shores to be despatched to Petrograd were simply incredible. Cranes brought load after load of fish from large flat-bottomed barges and dipped the round flat basket full of silvery, fretting fish into the ship's hold. We counted the baskets multiplied by the average weight, enquired after the recent market prices in Petrograd – and dreamt of making a fortune on these fish, or at least of existing on this income since all our own fortunes and estates had been taken from us – without indemnities – by the Bolshevik government. The prospect of having a *pied-à-terre* in some village on the shores of the lake was very attractive, too, as it would mean getting out of the industrial centre, which was becoming more and more untenable. But all these plans and projects were soon shattered: decree after decree scuppered all independent plans by outlawing all private enterprise and private capital.

However, I had seen the lake, I had crossed it in one of the passenger steamers leaving Petersburg every morning to steam up the Neva for about 70 kilometres and crossing the lake then towards the mouth of the river Svir, from west to east, a crossing lasting some six or seven hours, whereby for two hours no land could be sighted. And then the impressions left by the stretches of reeds, by the wide powerful Svir, by the constant herds of wild duck, geese and other waterfowl flying before and after sunset towards the night quarters – all this had fired my imagination and, fish or no fish, I wanted to try my luck shooting on the lake.

Fortunately two of my shooting friends shared my ideas and, being all young and rather vague about the possible turn of revolutionary progress, we keenly set to work to organise the shooting expedition we were dreaming of. The difficulties we had to overcome were very novel, unexpected, and perhaps the more interesting, as to carry out our plans *in spite* of everything gave it the more charm. First of all we had to legalise our possession of firearms and ammunitions, for several decrees had ordered the delivery of all arms without exception. Obviously we had not obeyed the first decrees and when the Bolshevik government came to power one of my friends and I had succeeded in obtaining an all-round permit for carrying arms and ammunitions (a rather unique document which, to my distress, was stolen with my pocket book in a crowded tram in Moscow a couple of years later). This permit, however, had value in Petrograd only, so a reason for taking arms to the Ladoga had to be found and permits for those parts could not be obtained easily.

One of us had this bright idea: we would join some cooperative organisation which were cropping up in masses then, we would suggest delivering to this organisation all sorts of game – a tempting proposition for anyone, as Petrograd was starving, and in exchange the organisation was to help us in receiving all necessary permits – shooting and travel included. Very soon the cooperative was found: one in our part of the town, with, as its president, a former butler who had been in the service of one of our uncles. Everything worked beautifully: the butler was only too pleased to give his gracious patronage to a nephew of his former rather haughty master, and secured for all three of us the required permits. In exchange we promised to deliver him every time we had been out shooting a couple of brace of duck, which we suspected went straight to his house and his large family and never found their way to the cooperative. How happy we were to be in possession of these duly stamped and pompously worded permits. They meant for us more than just the permission to shoot, for they gave us a civil standing; we were no longer unemployed former aristocrats and bourgeois living on the remnants of their fortunes and obstructing the clear air of the new revolutionary era. No – we were employed by a new social body and we had our proper identity papers, which really meant a lot at the time. We were working people and as such could claim the weekly herring and the daily piece of bread unashamedly.

It all sounded marvellous and, in fact, amusement aside, helped each of us in some way and gave us above all a certain feeling of security. Through the men on the steamer we got in touch with one or two villages near the Svir mouth and, having contacted the gamekeeper one of us already knew there, we set out one warm July morning on our official errand.

A long and restful trip, all up the Neva with the impressive and gloomy fortress of Schlusselburg at the entrance to the lake, large barges, few Remorqueurs, scarcely any steamers or other boats. Then, throughout the afternoon, the crossing of the lake, first along its southern shores, low marshy land with very few villages in sight, from time to time a glimpse of the important canal that runs at a small distance from the shore and which was built to allow the passage of barges throughout the year and when the navigation on the lake is rendered difficult because of constant violent storms. It looked strange to see steamers and barges gliding lazily and noiselessly through the grass as it looked from the distance. By three or four o'clock we were far from the shores and soon all traces of land disappeared. The sun was hot, we lay on the slanting roof of the passenger deck, having received the gracious authorisation of the captain, a nice grey-bearded old man.

Suddenly my attention was attracted by a quaint low line on the horizon and another one near it. "Submarines," I thought, "But it is ridiculous, here, in the lake!" I pointed them out to my friend who had been dozing.

"Submarines! Ridiculous . . . but," and he quickly rose to his feet. Yes, unmistakably they were submarines. We turned round to look at the captain on the bridge. He was just putting down his telescope, and to our gesture in that direction he only shook his head and shrugged his shoulders. "I must find out what we should expect," said my friend and walked off to talk to the captain. Coming back in a few minutes with a worried look on his face he said, "We might have luck as the fellows seem to be having a great washing day and are lazing about on deck, but they might want to board us for revision, and . . . well, one never knows how far our identity papers will satisfy those fellows. Red sailors are, after all, red sailors, even when they hide from the Allies' navy in these back waters!"

We spent an unpleasant quarter of an hour, with signalling going on, with our engines slowing down. And then came some cheerful waving from across the submarines, our engines put up speed again and I saw the captain lifting his cap and wiping the sweat off his forehead. Poor old man, maybe he was not all too revolutionary to stand safely control visits and passengers list checks.

The rest of the journey went on smoothly. The sunset was magnificent over the big expanse of water, which looked now like molten metal with the red blazing ball slowly disappearing into it. The evening was mellow and light, and we could enjoy to its fullest the lovely picture of the Svir opening up into the lake with its grey-green gently waving curtains of reeds hiding the shores on both sides. Soon the first villages became visible and in the clear evening light of a northern white night we landed.

The so-called gamekeeper we had been corresponding with was waiting for us near the landing stage. We got into his small rowing boat and half an hour later were at the foot of a small sandy cliff with a tiny jetty overlooked by a couple of houses. A boiling samovar was expecting us in the large room, fresh milk, bread and butter and boiled eggs looked extremely tempting after a long day of sandwich-eating. We soon settled for the night as the day's shooting was to start very early next morning. The *izba* was clean – to look at – the benches on which we slept were white, wooden and well washed, but in my tiny little room next door as well as in the large one where my friends slept there were such masses of fleas that none of us had a proper rest. Still, it was comforting to be far from town, not to wait half consciously for a house-search, not to dream of arrests. And then there was the prospect of tomorrow's sport – and certainly it was not a disillusion in any respect.

Lake Ladoga II: Duck Shooting

My second hunting trip to Lake Lagoda was in August 1918. Drizzly rain and cold wind reminded one of the approaching autumn. We had just reached the Nicolas station in Petersburg and were trying to get out to the evening train, which was to depart for Murmansk at about ten. The usual disorder, noise and nervousness prevailed, and it seemed only the more depressing as the cold deep air blurred the scanty light of the station lamps and gave the bustling crowds a ghostly appearance. The crowds were erring; no one really knew the destinations of the trains, and still greater vagueness prevailed with regard to their times of departure. There were no written indications anywhere – but to the majority of the crowd, most of whom were peasants and illiterate, this would not have been of much help.

The revolution had spread well over the country now. The Soviets held the power in their hands and a new order was being enforced upon the country with ruthlessness and total disregard of all former principles, usages, traditions – not to speak of former legislation. Everything was to be evened out, everything had to be knocked down so as to leave space for the new building – that of pure socialism and communism.

The upper classes were the first to suffer, and we had already been deprived of our property – the estates first, then the town houses, then bank accounts, bank deposits and safes. We remained thus without any sources of revenue and the vain hope of seeing things settle in some way that would allow us a possibility of existing. In the meantime, however, it was a real hand-to-mouth existence, with the daily expectation of some new "legal" blow and, worse still, the dread of imprisonment and all its consequences for officers, landowners, functionaries and civil servants. Having a well-known name or a title was already enough to make you suspect.

However, the worst was yet to come, we were still young, and the old passion for sport could not be killed right away. Therefore, two friends of ours and myself decided to try our luck with waterfowl on the Ladoga Lake. In exchange for a gallon of vodka a parish granted us the right of shooting in a more or less unlimited area at the mouth of the river Svir and along the adjacent shores of the lake in its south-eastern part.

The usual problem facing us was the guarantee that our guns and cartridges would not be taken from us by some local public safety committee, communist cell or any other more or less official authority. However, we had our arrangement with the cooperative and our "papers", with their array of seals and signatures, affording us the status of professional hunters in the region – an invaluable asset at the time. We also bribed one of the sub-managers of the train company with a couple of duck in return for the right to a small compartment in the sleeping car, which was otherwise reserved for the "high officials" of the Soviet government.

Thus, well provided with our impressive "documents", our baggage, a good supply of cartridges, our guns strapped over our shoulders and my Browning in my pocket, we made our way towards the train with plenty of time to slip into our reserved compartment before the government officials turned up. Everything went smoothly. The conductor turned out to be quite amenable and of the old school, as our little bribe worked wonders; the compartment was clean, well supplied with candles and even with water in the washstand. We settled down for the night, counting upon an early arrival at the small station, from where we had to go good twenty miles with horses.

The night was remarkably undisturbed – suspiciously quiet, I thought, as I peeped through the window in the early morning when we seemed to stop for quite a long time at some station. Strangely enough, the buildings I saw looked very familiar to me, and I soon realised that we had never moved from Petersburg. Just as we were discussing whether it would be wise to venture out (the conductor had advised us to remain as much as possible in our compartment, as there were crowds of officials who clamoured for separate compartments) the train gave a long dismal whistle and pulled off.

After this loss of a good day's sport, we arrived late at night in the small village on the banks of the Svir, where we rented the top floor of a peasant's house. The samovar was soon on the table, black bread, fresh salted butter, milk, jam and boiled eggs followed, and all were very welcome after the twenty-four-hour journey. The wind, which had been raging all day, seemed to have quieted down, and we hoped to have better weather the next day. The two men who kept their boats at our disposal were waiting for us. One was a local poacher and consequently knew best where the game was to be found. The other was a man of non-descript activities – as I found out later, he had just been released from gaol and was renowned locally as a very deft thief.

We left at dawn; my friend in a rowing boat with the thief, myself in a canoe with the poacher. A light breeze allowed us to put up our sails and we were soon beyond the port, the large sawing mills, the lines of low wooden huts, the stacks of timber; everything was wooden here, and the air was penetrated with the healthy scented smell of pine and birch. Once we were out in the open the shores were soon hidden in endless stretches of reeds. We parted here, agreeing to meet at midday on a certain island in the river Svir.

The sails were rolled up and we proceeded to enter this world of greys and greens, drifting through a wall of swaying reeds. I had as guide and gamekeeper a man who I had only seen for a moment on the evening of our arrival. He was not exactly prepossessing, I thought. Dark-eyed and with a scanty dark beard, his cap drawn down over his forehead and a darned and ragged coat hanging on his vaulted shoulders. He looked gloomy and morose and certainly he was not talkative. My friend had seemed reluctant to let me go with this man, but it turned out that he owned the better and safer canoe, so I had to go with him because of this. Of course I soon forgot the man as ducks rose up in flocks and I was kept very busy all the time. The gamekeeper had an excellent eye and deftly wound his way through the reeds to pick up the fallen birds – we never lost one. He had a nasty trick of finishing them off by biting through their necks – it was too unpleasant to look at. But he was certainly efficient, quick and silent. By midday we had a good bag and reached the island in good time.

The breeze had freshened and rather low clouds were now hurrying in from the west. After a quick lunch and rest we decided. My friend had told me of geese that he had seen in the distance but his gamekeeper, our landlord, was not certain where they could have come from. My silent man, when asked, murmured something unintelligible and we dropped the subject. However, as soon as we had set out again he suggested going to look for the geese.

"You know where they are?" I asked eagerly.

"Well I know, by chance, not so far, across the Svir, there," he said, pointing vaguely in a north-westerly direction.

"All right, let us go then!" I answered, delighted at the prospect of having a shot at geese.

The crossing of the Svir was quite easy as we were partly in the shelter of a bend, and once on the other side we made our way along the reeds towards the opening into the lake and delved soon into the sea of reeds where no sign of land could be seen. Ducks rose, I shot, the man pushed the boat to pick up the birds but kept standing up on his seat scanning the horizon.

"What are you looking for?" I asked.

"For my landmark to find the way towards the geese."

A landmark here? It seemed a most improbable thing to find, and when I finally asked him what it was he said, "A darkened spot of reeds – and there it is," and he swerved the canoe to the left. I abstained from shooting at the next ducks that flew out, my man nodded in silent approval. And then the geese rose, several of them at once. They seemed to cover the sky with their great outspread wings and their call seemed deafening to me, though I am certain they did not make much noise except with the whistling of their wings. How I shot, I could never remember, only I knew I had fixed on one goose, ignoring the others, and that goose fell with the dull noise of a heavy body landing with a big splash.

"Good shot! It's the old gander!" called out my guide, beaming all over his morose face and showing more excitement than I had thought him capable of. "Good," he repeated as he pushed the canoe fast into the reeds towards the fallen bird. It was a beauty and, to my relief, dead (so no need of the revolting bite in the neck, I thought).

Could we follow the flock? Any chance of approaching it again? We decided that such efforts would be wasted, the youngsters seemed to be big enough, and with the low cloud now running fast and darkening the sky we would not have time to scour the celebrated *guba* or gulf, thickly overgrown with reeds where the geese had probably sought shelter. Leisurely, resting on our laurels, we proceeded more or less towards the home village and I shot quite a few ducks as they rose in front of us. It had got grey and murky, the wind seemed to blow harder, though we did not really feel it in the shelter of the reeds. It had become colder too, and I began to feel my knees as I had been kneeling all day in the bottom of the canoe to have more freedom in turning right and left for shooting. As we approached the edge of the reeds a gust of wind startled me. I noticed a shadow on my guide's face as he pushed his cap down over his ears.

"Where shall we cross the Svir?" I asked now, wondering a little about this crossing. The Svir had seemed a big expanse of swiftly running water as we crossed it soon after noon and I had a slight feeling that conditions had turned for the worse.

"We'll have to try here, some fifty yards further, and we'll have to hurry for it will be getting dark much earlier today."

These words did not cheer me particularly, and when we swung out of the protection of the rushes into the open I certainly did not feel very courageous.

"You better leave the gun now and take the rudder. Point across, on a slant with the waves," he added, giving a swift glance to the water running high now in the river. The wind was howling now, the white-crested waves were whipped up with the current, being met here with the water driven against it by the westerly gale.

"We have no keel," I thought, and something similar must have crossed my guide's mind, as he quickly crossed himself before turning the canoe out into the open.

It was a nasty crossing. I shall never forget it. The waves were running fast, the wind was blowing very hard and the canoe seemed to dance quite aimlessly on this angry stretch of leaden-coloured, blackish water. I hung as fast as I could onto my rudder with the sickening feeling that it did not have any effect in these waves, it was more often out of the water than in it. My hands got numb, the spray of the white-crested waves showered a fine, damp spray all over us and the canoe danced in a most vagrant way which was, at times, quite terrifying.

"Hold on tight," called out my sinister guide, "and keep the boat steady half-way across the waves."

Of course I had to do my best, but it was not easy, and it seemed that we did not make any progress as each oncoming wave threw us back yards again. How long it took us to cross the river I really cannot tell, but it was getting dark when we finally reached the opposite wall of rushes and, diving into them, found suddenly a respite from the wind.

"Thank God!" said my guide making the sign of the cross, drawing in his oars and wiping his forehead, "It was not easy!"

Certainly, it was not easy, and my limbs felt like wooden clogs now, cold, lifeless and terribly clumsy. And it was cold – or was it because of the wet clothes which seemed now to cling to my body.

"Shall we get on towards the village or towards the island first?" I asked, just to say something and to hear a comforting word.

"We can't get to the village tonight – it is too late – the island is nearer," and my guide pushed now through the reeds and I sat doing nothing.

It grew dark, I grew colder and more numb and indifferent until a bright spot of light loomed between the reeds. "Look, a fire!" I called out, happy at the sight of the flames which promised welcome warmth.

"That's it – the island, and they made a fire there to guide us!" answered my guide, and his voice too sounded warmer. We pulled on, the fire grew bigger, and at last we landed on the inland where my friend was waiting anxiously for us.

"We've got a goose," I said weakly in response to his reproaches for being out so late. The tea brought life into my numb body, the fire cheered me, and, buried to my neck under the only haystack on the island, I slept like a log.

Lake Ladoga III: Mushroom Picking

It was a quiet, grey day by the lake. There were only two canoes available so one of us three guns had to stay on shore, and as I had been out all the previous days I generously offered to remain on land and to find some way of spending this last day we had at our disposal on the Svir and Ladoga. The wife of my guide, the sinister looking man, had already suggested my going for mushrooms in the big forests looming at the edge of the fields, and as I loved looking for mushrooms in new places I willingly agreed to her suggestion.

We set out in the morning, as soon as the men had gone in the canoes, and walked the two miles across the fields chatting about local life and conditions in the country. I avoided carefully anything more or less political – anything, I mean, that could be connected with the revolution – and the woman seemed entirely engrossed in her village interests. She was not one of those pleasant northern Russian women who I knew so well from our villages near Petersburg; she had something reserved about her, a certain scarcity of words not frequently found among village women. After a good two-hour search for mushrooms in one of the most magnificent fir tree forests I ever saw, where daylight penetrated reluctantly as if not to disturb the seclusion of the semi-darkness under the trees, we decided that it was time to have a rest and perhaps some tea. By this time we had been joined by another older woman and a young girl with rosy cheeks and bright, laughing eyes. The girl was making fun of the two other women, teasing them about having forgotten the best places for mushrooms and boasting about her two full baskets, which she could barely drag along. My companion, let us call her Anissia, made a few sour remarks in answer to her jokes and quickly put an end to the girl's high spirits – in fact, quicker than I would have expected.

The women invited me to come to their village and, as I had plenty of time before the men returned at three and we were to drive to the distant station for the six o'clock train, I agreed and went with them. The village was a nice typical north Russian village with two rows of rather high log *izbas*, the window frames nicely carved, the courtyards surrounded by a fence, a few flowers, mostly sunflowers, adorning the front space between the actual street – an earth-beaten track – and the *izba*.

Anissia was an excellent hostess and our samovar was steaming and singing in no time. Tea, with a few caramels instead of sugar, was most welcome and the excellent rye pancakes filled with potato purée and taken hot out of the oven were simply delicious. It made me think of my old Niania who was from the very north and who could make excellent pancakes and buns out of the simplest rye flour with sour milk and a little butter. So we chatted about cooking along these lines, and about the potato harvest, and the best way to prepare mushrooms.

The young girl left us soon as her mother was expecting her to be home before she returned from the fields, and I remained alone with Anissia and her friend – a most unprepossessing dirty looking woman. Anissia went on talking and every time I made signs of leaving she tried to stop me and put in new questions about things and life in Petrograd. I did not quite like it, I felt there was something unnatural about this very keen interest, and besides, I wanted to be back on time so as to pack my bag and not delay the others. Finally, with great difficulty, I managed to free myself of Anissia's conversation and walked off at a rapid pace to our village, which fortunately lay some two miles across the fields. Somehow, I preferred the idea of walking across the fields, somewhere where I saw the road clearly before me. Only later did I understand my instinctive feeling about Anissia.

I reached the village just as the men were landing with a very good bag and during a quick meal with the hosts before leaving they asked me what I had been doing.

"I went with Anissia to look for mushrooms in that large forest to the north-east of here, and we found lots – I have a basket full of them to bring home," I answered triumphantly, adding that I had had tea at Anissia's house before coming back here. There were no comments about my doings, but after tea our host, whose name was Shennikov, when helping me to pack my gun and tie up the game suddenly took me by the arm.

"Don't you go too much with Anissia, she is not a reliable woman, one never knows what might happen . . ."

I was astonished and naturally asked what it was about.

Hesitatingly, and obviously reluctantly, our host told me, "Anissia has only just returned from Siberia . . . she was convicted there for participating in a murder. Her mother was the guilty one. They cut the throat of a peddler who had asked for shelter one dark autumn night . . . one never knows . . . she may be all right, of course, but . . ."

I thanked him for the warning and thought it advisable to add that I always carried my Browning with me and that I knew pretty well how to handle it.

A bright smile illuminated Shennikov's face, "That's right, you are the right sort, God protects those who are ready to protect themselves," and all at once his worried look vanished.

From then on I knew I was safe when I came to these far-off places, probably safer even than the men, as a woman with a pistol must have been something pretty special in the eyes of the local inhabitants.

Shennikov

Shennikov interested us more and more. The man was helpful and very quiet, in fact silent, but when he did talk he always had something to say. I think he rather liked us as sportsmen since we were not afraid of bad weather, absence of roads or rather precarious sleeping quarters. Perhaps, too, he had never come across a woman who shared in all these difficulties without causing any special trouble. Anyhow, on the third day of our sport together he became more communicative and very clearly gave way to his own thoughts and feelings, apparently glad to talk over things with people who liked to hear him talk and who would not give him away to the nearest local communist cell.

As we were sailing in the afternoon to the bank of rocks he had spoken of as the best place to get the migrating duck, he inquired casually about our life and occupations and seemed interested and glad to hear that we were both landed proprietors – and not merely Petersburg citizens in quest of new fun.

"Landed proprietors," he said suddenly, "they are not in the picture now – and you don't mind saying you are one of them. I am glad, and there are many of them I knew and respected. They stand their own ground, if they are the right sort of landed proprietor."

This sounded so simple and clear – and so understandable that I immediately felt quite at home with him and we chatted happily about the country and about sailing, too, as I had always been interested in sailing ever since I first tried it on the Italian Riviera at the age of eight or nine. Shennikov sat at the rudder guiding his broad, well-set barge in a rather awkward westerly wind which did not exactly help us on our course. His cap deep over his eyes, which looked red and wind-blown, the collar of his coat lifted and his powerful body riveted to the narrow plank at the rudder, he looked the type of a *loup de mer* as I had always imagined them to be.

"Look here, Shennikov," asked my friend suddenly, "have you always sailed in these parts for fishing only?"

Shennikov smiled into his beard. "Yes, fishing at all times – as far as the weather permitted it, but not only fishing. One does not make much money out of the fishing in these waters, you know."

I could well imagine it, for I had heard of the scarcity of fish in these parts of the Finnish Gulf. "But you must have shared your time between fishing and agriculture?" I put in, "For your fields round the village look well looked after and in perfect condition."

Shennikov gave me a beaming smile. "It is good to hear that someone appreciates the look of the fields. My two sons have put a lot of work into it since I could not carry on with the ploughing – I broke my leg and never got it quite straight again. Yes, the fields are some of the best in these parts of the county," and he gave a pleased look over his shoulder to the vanishing line of fields behind us.

"But could you make a living on these fields?" asked my friend rather bluntly and certainly not diplomatically, I thought.

Shennikov seemed to take it very simply, "No, we could not live – as we wanted to – on these fields, nor on the fishing, which did help us a lot. We had other ways . . ." he smiled and shrugged his shoulders.

I was intrigued. "What did you do then to help out?" A most undiplomatic question, and I felt ashamed the moment I had uttered it. But our host did not seem to mind it.

"Well, we had some traffic with Finland – a regular traffic which brought us in enough money to live as we wanted to, my sons and myself."

I wondered, and my friend asked bluntly, "With Finland? What traffic can or could you have there? Across the Finnish Gulf? Do tell us, Shennikov."

Shennikov was obviously quite ready to talk freely to us (in fact we were alone in the barge as his nephew, the younger gamekeeper, was being towed in the small canoe behind our barge and tossed around to his heart's content – if such was his pleasure.

"Indeed, I have been across to Finland many hundreds of times. To tell you the truth, not many people know it, though some do make guesses about it," he added with a cunning smile. "I used to go over to bring salt and matches – they were cheaper over there; it was worthwhile and I took across whatever was useful, always different things and always worth trying. Yes, I did have my bit of fun out of it, dodging the picket boats and the customs men –they never caught me – and after all, my doings did not hurt anyone – apart from perhaps the *kasna* (the State finances, which were regularly looked upon in old Russia as the milking cow or the fool to be fooled)." He chuckled happily. "I did not hurt anyone," he repeated, "and I did get such a lot of fun out of it!"

There was the real sportsman speaking out freely. I loved him for this open-hearted sentence.

"Good for you, Shennikov! You must have had a lot of adventures during these crossings!" put in my friend, "And you must know every rock and every current playing in these waters."

"Well, I don't think there are many who know the places as well as I do – and that without maps," added Shennikov with self-complacency. "In many a storm I had to find my way with no maps and no lights – and avoiding the lighthouses too! And God always helped me out, so I really think my trade was not as wicked as all that. It was contraband, but after all, there was the big family to be seen to, and with the scarcity of fish and the insufficient income from the fields . . ."

"I would not mind crossing over to Finland with you," I put in casually, not thinking of what I was saying.

Shennikov turned to me quickly. "Do you think of it? If you do or ever think of doing it, let me know. I'll take you over as safely as one can – with God's blessing. Only let me know in time. And you would not be the first either."

This idea startled me. Yes, I may one day be in the position of wanting to get across – I did not know at the time how close to me that moment was – and I saw at once that this was an opportunity that could not be left unnoticed. "Thank you, Shennikov, I'll certainly ask you before anyone else – if I have to go across on the quiet."

We were silent for a time, then Shennikov put in casually, "Not long ago, one of our local landed proprietors had to go over – quickly. He was not persona grata with the new government, he was a man of the old stock, a real good landowner and we all loved him. Well, he came to me and we set out that very evening and got across safely in the moonless night – in summer it is easier – and he is over there and in safety, and this means a lot to any man!"

A wistful look on the bearded man's face really touched me. "Yes, to be in safety is something we never thought about – it was so natural – but now . . . it does mean more than we could ever imagine."

All three of us laughed as Shennikov added, "Doesn't it sound as though we were all three of us fugitives from the law, escapees from a prison?" It was a joke, but he did not know how closely he skimmed reality as things developed in the course of the next couple of years.

We were approaching the bank now – a row of low grey rocks, in fact breakwaters, against which the waves from the open sea ran furiously to break in rows of angry white crests and fountains of spray. From our side, the inland approach, the sea was comparatively quiet and as we came closer we saw that the rocks were literally covered with duck, studded with birds of all varieties to be found in our northern waters. But they were careful and we could not approach them within shot that evening. They flew high above our heads, circling over the bank, disappearing towards the east, for Shennikov said that there were more and smaller banks of rocks in that direction. We could only look and admire and hope for a chance of shooting in the early hours of the morning when the same birds flew low over the water and circled over our bank, as Shennikov said, for it was their rallying point before turning south after the sun had risen for good.

A year later, Shennikov agreed to take me illegally across the border towards Finland when I was trying to get out of Russia to join my children. Money was not worth much at the time and I had offered to leave him one of my guns. He took the offer willingly and was to bring me in his canoe across the Svir to the places I knew where the wild geese nested. There I was to land on a sandbank which ran north among the reeds for a distance of about twelve miles and at the end of it I had to wade through shallow water, dodging a village (which meant wading by night), until I reached a sandy cliff where I would already be in Finland. It was not exactly an easy task, but with the prospect of reaching my children all tasks seemed feasible, and I readily agreed to this plan.

A week before the proposed escape, Shennikov came to Petrograd to tell me that he could not undertake to take me over because a strong garrison of red army soldiers had been posted in the village situated at the end of the sandbank, and there was no chance for me to get past their posts into Finland. I thanked him warmly for the warning and especially for all the trouble he had taken in coming all the way to Petrograd. A good selection of cartridges was the most welcome pay he could have, and we parted great friends, never to meet again.

THE COACHMEN
AND
THE GAMEKEEPER

10

IVAN THE GAMEKEEPER AND THE COACHMEN

For many years my three small boys were firmly convinced that a coachman was inevitably called Ivan. It was an axiom for them: all coachmen had to be called Ivan – although perhaps they knew that not all Ivans were coachmen. The fact is that the coachmen they knew best in their early childhood were all three Ivan, and all three were devoted to our family. The boys certainly had good reason to consider all "coachmen Ivan" as friends, besides admiring them as the greatest authorities on horses, stables, and carriages. Somehow the feeling that a coachman called Ivan is a friend just because he has that name caught me too and even now, after scores of years without any sort of coachman, I still subconsciously believe that once a man dealing with horses is blessed with this name, he must obviously be a good man. Maybe I think this because I have not had a coachman for over thirty years now – and have not been disillusioned! Who knows?

As I look back into the past I visualise all these three Ivans and also their respective horses and feel I must write down for the boys' sake what I remember of their first friends, and my old devoted friends. Maybe I had better start with the oldest in the line, the one who was my first friend when I was a child and whose picture is very vivid in my mind.

Coachman Ivan of Petersburg

Ivan was our coachman in Petersburg when I was a child. We had at the time a pair of really good grey trotters in Petersburg. My father was very pleased with them and I thought they were the best pair in town, except, perhaps, the Emperor's horses, just because he was the Emperor. I did not know which I liked better, Sizyi or Bystryi, as the first was perhaps a little stronger and slightly lazy, whereas the second was full of spirit, a little nervous but seemed to get more easily tired, which was natural for a nervous horse. Anyway, they looked splendid when used separately in a small, very light sledge or as a pair with the larger sledge and the dark blue heavy net spread over their backs to prevent clumps of snow flying at us when the horses were at full trot. And how proud Ivan was when he stopped his pair at the steps, the reins tightly drawn, his arms outstretched, his red beard spreading like a fan over his broad chest, his stately figure in the navy blue livery, his fur-lined coat and the coloured tape girdle wound round the middle, and the small elegant leather case with a clock stuck into the girdle at the back for us to see the time without having to open our fur coats or taking off our gloves.

It was a great joy when father came into our schoolroom and called me to have a short ride with him. How proud I was that he wanted me and how I enjoyed in advance all the stories he would tell me as we drove, stories of horses, perhaps of ice-yachting or the story of some old houses we might be passing. He always found something thrilling to tell me and I rarely could repeat the stories to my governess because I was sure she would not appreciate them and would not feel how lovely these stories were when told as we passed the places, as the icy cold wind blew and pricked my face, as the snow flew in clumps from under the strong swift hoofs of the greys. Father hid his face in his beaver collar, I put my fur muff against one cheek, then against the other, to prevent them from freezing, hiding behind Ivan's broad back as he stood there erect, solid as a pyramid, immovable except for the slight bend of an arm or the deep bass call of "beregi-is!" (Get out of the way!) when someone crossed the street too slowly, or "derzhi pravey-i!" (Move over to the right!) when he wanted to pass another sledge. And what I loved was to hear Ivan add to this call "rybolov!" when we passed a closed carriage with an English harness and the coachman in a top hat with his whip fixed upright in front of him and which Ivan called "the fishing rod"! – I always laughed when I heard it, father smiled and made as if he had not heard. And the snow creaked and whizzed under the steel sleighs and we slid slightly when taking the corners, just a slight skidding movement, for more would have been bad driving on the part of Ivan, and the sledge flew so smoothly, so noiselessly but for the willing steady stamping of the horse.

Then father would tell Ivan where we wanted to stop. I could usually guess where: the big confiseries of Conradi on the Nevsky for sweets for us children, or at Bellets for special candied fruit my mother liked, and then, already nearly home, when I counted with regret the last turnings of streets, father would stop at "Fleurs de Nice", the first original fresh flower shop established by two brothers, Frenchmen from the South of France. How well Ivan could stop the horse, dead still, their hoofs dug like stubborn toes into the snow, every sinew of their legs tight and tense, light steam hovering over their bodies, their necks bent, swanlike, only their sensitive ears trembling slightly and their wide open nostrils blowing freely the "clouds of smoke", as I called them.

We got out of the sledge then, drawing our feet out of the fur bag in which they had kept so warm and throwing back the fur rug held in place by two thick navy-blue cords forming two loops and each adorned with a heavy tassel. Down the steps into the shop, upon opening the double doors we were met by an unexpected mild spring-scented air in this whitewashed, plain-walled basement. Plain, that is, but for the masses of cut flowers in wide earthenware basins, in high slim vases and foreign-looking terracotta jars, this mass of flowers of all colours and tints and scents was a tremendous contrast with the white, cold, silvery sight that had given me such joy during our drive. These flowers carried me away to Italy, which had made a huge impression upon me every time I went there in spring with my mother. I tried to remember the names of the flowers, and I always forgot them because it was so much nicer and familiar to know them as stars and double stars on short and long legs – know them as I connected them with the places I had seen them grow.

The orders were given; the Frenchmen arranged all the flowers in our house, but at times father liked to see for himself what looked best at the moment, or what tints he would like in particular for the dinner party tomorrow, or the birthday party a couple of days later. Armed with a large white paper parcel in which were wrapped in a thin layer of cotton wool some roses or carnations that Father wanted my mother to have right away on our return, we left the shop and got back into the sledge for the short drive home.

Before going up the steps I always managed to pat the horse, to tell Ivan how I enjoyed the drive, how well he left behind the "fisherman with the rod". These greys were a link between Ivan and myself, for otherwise I had no opportunity to speak to him, as we children were not allowed down into the yard or the stables, nor into the kitchen or servants' quarters where Ivan had his meals with the other servants.

However, things were not always as smooth and easy with Ivan, and at times I saw my father frown when mother told him something about Ivan not being too sober last night. It was the first time in my life that I realised that someone I knew and liked could be drunk, that in this state accidents could happen, and that it was so bad to be drunk that one did not talk about it.

I had seen lots of drunken people, peasants or poorly dressed people, especially on Sundays, tottering down the streets, and I had watched with great interest and a real thrill how people sidled along the pavement, zigzagging with a nice, soft-legged walk and rounded arm movements, brushing the wall with their shoulder to be ricocheted to the lamp post. It had been quite a private little sport of mine to see whether or not the interesting individual would run into this heap of snow instead of finding himself embracing the lamp post, or whether he'd avoid the protruding steps of the large entrance door opposite us, or whether he would be ricocheted right into the door of a little fruit shop that did not seem to close on Sundays. It was quite an exciting sport, and when I could get my brother to keep me company on the windowsill behind the double windows we had a regular gamble over it. But there was one thing I hated and dreaded and invariably closed my eyes for, to be teased by my brother about it, and that was when the "individual" with cotton wool legs was making a beeline for the treacherous steep steps of the tobacco shop down in the basement right opposite us. It was a breath-taking moment; I pictured the poor man rolling down these icy, slippery stone steps with no bannister to hold on to, and I seemed to hear his shouts of distressed calls for help. It was simply terrifying! However, it never happened, not once! When I could summon up the courage listening to my brother saying "Don't be stupid, he won't roll down, look there," I saw the man sidle swiftly towards the abyss and on the edge of it, he'd suddenly stop, bend down his head perhaps in a querying gesture and sway with a jerk in the other direction to land on the snow heap or slide into the road itself or embrace and hug the lamp post. It was a huge relief, something people must enjoy when they see a horror film nowadays. Why the man always escaped was a problem I could not solve, but old Niania had once told me: "Don't worry, there is God who protects the drunkards!" and this made me think naturally that a drunkard cannot be really too bad a man if God looks after him, and this feeling remained even when I could reason out the problem in another light.

But at the time, when mother spoke about Ivan and father frowned and knitted his black eyebrows and told the footman to call him, I did not really understand why the atmosphere was so serious, why there was a black cloud. And then one day I was passing through the room when father was speaking to Ivan. Father had his serious voice and his serious look and Ivan looked sad, nodding, nodding. The next day, as my sister and I were going out for the daily walk with our governess, I felt someone touching my sleeve and turning round I saw Ivan, in "civilian" clothes, looking so unimpressive without the cushion padding of his livery.

"Miss," Ivan was saying, "do be a kind child, ask His Excellency to take me back. I won't drink anymore, true I won't. Do ask. His Excellency, Edy, please . . ." and he mumbled something more that I could not hear as my governess had turned round and was pulling me by the arm. I had only time to say, "Yes, Ivan, of course I won't forget." And I didn't forget and father listened to me and smiled and Ivan was back.

This happened several times, again when I was older and quite realised the danger we all ran when Ivan sat on the box of the closed carriage barely holding the reins of the restless pair – not the greys anymore, generally the blacks. I understood father's anger and mother's nervousness, but still, Ivan had always been so good with the horses and he knew them so well, and by then I appreciated the way he handled them with art and a sure hand. It was a weakness of Ivan's, but all coachmen seemed to have it – in winter, at least – and it was quite understandable when they had to wait for us for hours on end in the hard and biting frost. And every time Ivan returned after a dramatic interview with my father, I smiled up at Ivan when I saw him again on the box and he gave me a slight nod or muttered a "thank you" when I slipped to the horses' heads to pat their velvety noses whilst mother was getting into the carriage and having the fur wrapped round her legs by the porter or the footman.

* * *

Years went by. Father had another coachman, I don't remember why. I grew up, I married and had my own coachman Ivan in my country place, and the memory of the red-bearded Ivan vanished from my head. Then the revolution broke out; our estate was taken and I found myself alone in my town house having to face an interview with the "communist commandant" of our block of houses in order to settle something about the house and new communist "decrees" and ordinances.

I was alone and had to handle all these new problems cropping up daily, all urgent, all unexpected, all without precedents and all finding me obviously quite unprepared and very vague, as there was no legal background to rely upon, no legal force to support us. In fact, everything seemed to be a matter of luck – or bad luck – often of quick thinking, of quick reaction. I felt all this instinctively but had certainly not worked it out cool-headedly and it probably would have been of no avail, anyhow. Thus, summoning up my courage and conscious of it being my duty to do all in my power to keep the house for my family, I went down the three flights of stairs and across the yard to the small door which had been pointed out to me as the dwelling of the new communist house commandant (the previous one had occupied a biggish flat). I knocked at the door, which was immediately opened by a small boy of about twelve. In the back of the room, which formed the flat with a tiny kitchen attached at the back, sat an older man bent over a pair of boots that he was polishing vigorously.

"Could I speak to the House commandant?" I asked the boy.

The man turned round abruptly, the red beard, and a beaming smile: "Edinka, Countess! Yes, here I am now, times have changed. Yes, I am the commandant, who could have thought it?" and he stood there with his broad smile and a strange wistful expression in his eyes.

I was so taken aback that I could not think what to say, how to address him. In a few words he told me how he had been appointed by the "new authorities" because his daughter-in-law knew them all (I quickly noted that, for it meant to keep well out of the way of that daughter-in-law) and finished by saying, "Times have changed, no greys, no blacks, I can just as well be a communist and be in the old house!"

This was an unexpected conclusion, but Ivan was here, Ivan could not have changed much and I could talk to him – probably – without fear. Cautiously I sketched out the situation, avoided mentioning my husband, who as an officer would be evidently "suspect" and who was at the moment somewhere "in hiding". Ivan only nodded his head, ordered his boy to note what I wanted with regard to the new decree, which had to be "walked round", frowned and stroked his beard, repeating: "We will see to it . . . We'll manage . . ." But I still hoped to think we were both friends, and I left soon fearing some stranger's call. As Ivan opened the door for me, he patted my shoulder and smiling childishly from under his bushy eyebrows said swiftly, "Come to me when you want help – I'll find the way to wriggle out!"

How relieved I felt and what an utterly unexpected surprise it had been to see old Ivan, in this exalted position, after all the years that I had lost sight of him – to feel that he had remained a devoted old friend.

Ivan kept his word and helped me in a quiet, unnoticeable way throughout the two years that I remained entirely alone in my house in Petersburg. He was really my guardian angel, helpful and clever in getting on the right side of the "new law". At that he was illiterate, it was his little son who had to read out aloud every new decree, every new ordinance which came out for the old man to ponder over – and by the time I had read the paper and came down to ask him for advice, Ivan had already found an answer to the new difficulties.

Thus one morning instructions were issued (I fear I cannot use the technical legal term as I never quite followed them in the soviet administration) according to which so many square yards per head were allowed as living space, the surplus being at the disposal of the municipal authorities. In many well-to-do houses of the residential quarters entire families of factory workmen, groups of soldiers and sailors had already been billeted upon the owners, who were strictly assigned "living space". Worried by this prospect as only three rooms were occupied in my sixteen-room apartment, I went for advice to Ivan. He met me with a knowing smile which meant "I know what you've come for!" and added that he had just worked out a plan for me and was carrying it out. Pointing to his boy who was bending over house books and papers, Ivan said in a triumphant tone, "You see, Vaska is copying out of the house book the name of suitable people who died here in the course of the last few years. I will say they are alive and all live in your house. They are registered now as your tenants. Will that do?"

I was aghast. "Ivan dear, but this is marvellous! Shall I learn their names?"

"No, you go home and put in all the rooms some sort of a bed, hang up here a skirt, there a pair of trousers – well, you know, to show someone lives there – and if the authorities turn up, I will talk to them, that's better."

As I thanked him effusively, he gave me one of his broad placid smiles and said, "There it is, you'll have to live with the dead souls, they are not bad people – and very quiet tenants!"

They certainly were, and I never knew their names. Only in putting down coats and trousers, hats and shoes, stray brushes and shawls near the bedsteads arranged all over the place, I pictured to myself who these dead souls were and soon imagined their names and occupations as I thanked them in my head for the good turn they were doing me. True to his word, Ivan did all the necessary introductions when communist search parties appeared in the night to search the houses of this quarter of the town – search for people hiding, for money, jewels, firearms, photographic cameras, and a number of things the choice of which frequently depended upon the momentary inspirations of the members of the search party. Ivan walked in with the head of the party and rattled off by heart name after name of my "tenants" as he led the way from room to room. I was always mentioned by Ivan as the "hostess, who is the wife of a very good Red Air Force man now in Moscow". Once or twice I heard him explain the absence of my tenants, saying that several of them worked in a night shift in a factory, others had been sent to the province on a government job and someone was having a baby in hospital. So it all worked to perfection; the house search went its very unpleasant way, opening cupboards, pulling out drawers, unlocking boxes, throwing clothes out of cupboards to see whether weapons were hidden in the depths of these enormous old-fashioned linen and clothes cupboards. And after four or five hours of searching they would walk away with sleepy Ivan talking ponderously and patiently, unperturbed, unruffled, probably to continue the search in some other part of the building. What I marvelled at was Ivan's readiness on the spot with suitable answers, something one would least expect from an elderly men who had always been a coachman and who could not even read or write.

* * *

Another instance of Ivan's thoughtfulness occurs to me. It was in November, 1919, on a nice frosty and dry day. I had gone out soon after breakfast, consisting of a little black coffee without sugar and of some dry black bread, and was approaching home at about mid-day when I noticed in front of our gate a stationary motor car. I must explain here that there were no private cars left in the town at all; all were requisitioned for the army or the officials, and mainly for the Cheka. Thus a car was a rarity and generally an unpleasant one too. Having seen it from the distance, I crossed the road, and slowly passing my house on the other side of the street I noticed a dosing driver in it. Probably the car had arrived some time ago – why? – better not try to solve the mystery but wait – and I went on leisurely, looking over my shoulder from time to time. The car was still there. I turned round the block of houses and coming in sight of my house saw the same car at the door. Another walk, another unpleasant return, until I finally found the coast clear after having walked around for two hours. Cautiously I entered the gates: not a soul to be seen. I walked up the stairs and noisily passed my door, creeping back to it on tiptoes to hear whether there was any movement inside the house. No, everything quiet. With a beating heart I opened the door and found Masha, my former maid, tidying the room I had let to a nice old spinster, Baroness K.

"What a blessing you did not return earlier," exclaimed Masha. "They have been here all morning searching the room of the Baroness. They wanted to see you, and finally they took her away to the Cheka."

I was speechless. The Baroness? The quiet old spinster of sixty-two? Why, what for? Rushing down to Ivan for explanations, I was met with the same exclamation, "What a blessing that you did not come home earlier. The Cheka was in your house to get the Baroness, asking for you too. I just had time to order Vaska to watch for you from the stable door opposite the gate – he was to warn you as soon as you passed under the porch. They were here for over three hours."

Had Ivan not sent his boy to warn me I might have walked in and been taken too. I could not find out what the reason for the old lady's arrest could have been, and only many years later, in Paris, did I meet her sister who told me that the old lady was kept in prison for eight months, that she was released but in such poor health that she died soon afterwards. The reason for the arrest was that her brother-in-law, with whose widow I was speaking, had been a leader of the conservative party in the last Duma, could not be found in Petersburg in 1919 and so the old sister-in-law had to pay with her life.

* * *

Since 1917 I had been hiding our sports guns and our collection of old guns in the house in spite of decrees ordering the delivery of all arms to the authorities. A couple of the sports guns had been taken by the peasants when our estate was "nationalised" or simply taken by the people. The better guns, which were in the special care of Sidor the gamekeeper, had been hidden by him together with our coachman Ivan Kamenski from Kamenka, and the latter told me that he took them over to his own *izba* in the next village, some six miles away, and dug them into the ground under the floor. Still, there remained seventeen guns in Petersburg, about as many pistols and revolvers – an impressive arsenal as there were plenty of ammunition for the modern weapons. But I simply could not bring myself to deliver all these good clean weapons into the hands of the Bolsheviks; I felt it would be disloyal to these weapons, which might be used against innocent people or end up in the hands of people I despised or highly disapproved of. So I kept them, hiding them in a wall cupboard which was very unobtrusive in a passage and which I papered over myself, papering the whole wall of this passage.

In the end, when things got from bad to worse in Petersburg, I could not stand the strain of the secret, especially as the discovery during the frequent house searches would have brought disaster not only upon myself but upon the people around me, such as my maid Masha, my brother's old invalid friend to whom I had let a room, and also to Ivan, as he was responsible for the house, and the cunning web of stories he had wound around me for the sake of the officials would have come out in the end. Thus, after a renewed decree threatening the severest measures for non-delivery of arms, I went to Ivan and confessed to him my fears. He shook his head, patted his beard and told me that he would come to me when he had found a solution.

The same evening Ivan turned up at dusk (I think he did not want people to see that he went to my house, for people were all spying on each other and one never knew). He had devised a plan. By tomorrow evening all the weapons were to be wrapped up in rags, previously copiously oiled with paraffin – we had no other oil available – and he with his son and a nephew would come to fetch them. The nephew was to dig a deep hole under the log floor of our disused carriage house.

The next morning I opened my cache and worked hard at oiling, wrapping up and tying up each gun separately. At nightfall Ivan turned up with his help. We walked cautiously down the dark backstairs, slipped one by one into the carriage house, not daring to light a lantern until the door was closed, and the nephew slipped down into the deep trench where he could light the lantern without there being any danger of people seeing the light through chinks of the door. It was quickly done, the laying down of my favourites, the earth was thrown over them, the logs moved in place. I crept out before the others, my strength would not be much help and it was a painful moment. But Ivan was plucky to have run the risks, really for a whim of mine. Whether these arms are still there, I have always wondered. There is a good chance that they are, to judge by the last sign of touching devotion given me by Ivan five years after I left Russia.

* * *

I was working at the American International Reference Service in Paris and the head of our service (I shall refer to him as Mr X) was going to Russia to search for some publications he wanted (or so he said). I gave him my old address in Petersburg and the name and description of Ivan. On his return, my American friend gave me a full account of his visit to Ivan, who apparently was very uncommunicative at first and doubted whether the American was really coming in my name as a friend. Finally, when Mr X gave a description of myself and of my three boys, Ivan believed that we really were acquainted and asked for permission to call at the hotel the next day. When he turned up there, Mr X had to tell him in detail all that I was doing now and how I lived and earned for all of us, and finally, on taking leave, Ivan produced from the inner pocket of his jacket a double sheet of white paper on which was scribbled in pencil lists of things found in my house when the communists took possession of it. He added, "I thought she would like to know what there was remaining there – not much, you know, still if she came back . . ."

Poor Ivan, he had tears in his eyes, said Mr X, and when they shook hands, Ivan kissed the American's hand, saying "for her". Perhaps this was the best little piece of propaganda in our favour, the old "ruling class", for it showed that we could not have been so hated after all. I still have the list – in the son's clumsy rough handwriting – a list of such incongruous and useless things, probably the little remaining that had not been disposed of by Masha and her friends.

It was hard never to be able to write even a few words to Ivan, but I dare not write; a letter from abroad would have been noticed by everyone and might have put him in an awkward position. I only hope he knew of my lasting gratitude for all he did for me.

Coachman Ivan of Kamenka

Small and thin, with a shrivelled face and very bushy eyebrows, this coachman Ivan of Kamenka, our country place, had nothing of the presence of the Petersburg Ivan of old days. Silent and attentive, he went on with his work in a methodical, meticulous manner very rarely found among Russians. His low, deep voice seemed too important for so small and narrow-chested a man; he rarely raised it except against the stable boys who were, as a rule, haphazard workers, forgetful and lazy. "Unreliable," he used to say with a displeased shaking of his head. Strangely enough there was one, the youngest groom I ever saw – due to the revolution, we had no men on the farm and none could be found in the village; it was the ten-year-old Polish boy, Adamka, whose family had fled from Poland during the German advance and who I had taken on for the estate farm. Ivan had a kind smile for this thin-faced little boy who understood little Russian but seemed to guess what was wanted from him, but for whom the jokes about his age and size passed unnoticed. When Ivan called, "Adamka, get your stepladder and put the bridle on Sizyi," Adamka would take the bridle and deftly climb along the partition of the box, onto the hay rack and a minute later lead out, serious and dignified, the huge Sizyi and push him and back him into the shafts of the cart, and Ivan would smile and shake his head, repeating under his breath "Nal da udal" (Small but clever).

Ivan played a big part my boys' lives and he invariably appeared in Alec's prayers, whose love for horses made him concentrate all his attention on everything connected with the stables. But Ivan, though generally quiet, could be strict with my boys and would send them quickly enough out of the stables or the riding school if they got noisy or disobeyed him.

Ivan had a very definite idea, of what was right in the gentleman's stable or way of driving. I can't say that I quite shared his ideas about driving in particular, but he was so sure of the right thing to do that I simply had not got the courage to give him different orders. Thus he always insisted on driving at full speed downhill near the house and on putting the horses to full gallop across the bridge and up the hill. I weakly suggested once or twice that at the end of the 40 km drive the horses might be tired and this extra gallop might be too much for them – but the look of blame, of wondering disappointment in the eyes of Ivan made me soon understand that I must have said some heresy with regard to his code of driving and that there was nothing to be done since this was the "proper gentleman's way" of arriving home. I resigned myself and meekly suffered these noisy arrivals, the thundering on the wooden bridge, the terrifying swing left into the gate, with all the harness bells ringing madly, with the horses splashing through the pools or throwing clumps of snow and ice in all directions. To my distress the same pace was maintained when we passed through the long stretched village street of Tosno, near the railway station. I got very worried about this during the revolution when a less noticeable passage would have been safer – but Ivan could not change his ideas and I preferred taking risks than upsetting the poor man's old and solidly rooted principles.

I'll never forget the most spectacular of such drives. It was in winter and I had to go to the wedding of a young gamekeeper in the village church some 20 km from home. It was very cold and I hid my face and ears deep in my fur coat. When we approached the church Ivan turned off into the drive and suddenly bounced up, squaring his narrow shoulders, stretching out his small figure lost in the fur-lined livery coat of dark-green cloth, swinging his long whip and putting the tandem of horses into a frenzied gallop. With foaming mouths and panting hard, they stopped abruptly at the steps where crowds of villagers had assembled. "This was a proper arrival!" said Ivan turning round to me with such an expression of triumph and pride on his face that I could only agree with him and laugh inwardly, for I suddenly had a vision of similar noisy and flashy drives in Naples, in my early childhood, when the brandishing and cracking of whips by the local cabs had thrilled me.

* * *

During the war years I came more and more to respect the value of our local customs and superstitions, even when on occasions they made my task in managing the estate even harder than usual. One day I was sitting groaning over some dairy accounts when Ivan the coachman was shown into the study. He stood there, cap in hand, high felt boots just brushed from the snow, and indicating by his serious look that all was not well.

"My Lady, excuse me, but we must sell the new horse," he announced with a dignified assurance allowing no doubts.

"Sell the new horse? But why? Have you tried it again this morning? Is it ill?" I could not see why the horse I had bought only the day before – upon Ivan's special advice, and after due tests – should now be sold without having been used. The animal had given entire satisfaction when we drove home, the long 30 versts drive from the station; it had shown no signs of fatigue, had looked fit and ready to go on although we had driven rather fast.

"It won't do – it doesn't suit us," replied Ivan looking steadily at the ceiling.

Ivan had something on his mind, it was clear, but I could not imagine what it was. "I can't make it out, Ivan. Tell me what the matter is. I will sell it if you explain what it's all about."

"The horse can't stay in our stables. 'He' won't have him," whispered Ivan looking furtively around. Now I understood. "He" – in other words the spirit of the stables – did not approve of our new purchase. Was it the colour, I wondered? Every stable

179

or farm is said to have favourite colours – those that please the local spirit. No, the horse was light brown and Ivan had said this colour would be suitable. What was it that had gone wrong? Apparently the horse had been in a dreadful lather because "He" had been sitting on the horse's back and "torturing" it all night long.

I went with Ivan to the stables. We found the sturdy, well-built brown horse eating peacefully as if nothing had happened. But its coat certainly showed signs of the lather it had been in.

It would have been no use at all to try to persuade Ivan to change his mind. However loath I was, I had to sell the horse – and that at a moment when we really needed it very much and had little time to look for another. Gazing at the ceiling and spitting (with due respect to my presence) into the corner, Ivan remained steady in his certainty that the horse did not please the spirit and therefore it must go, or evil would befall the stables and us.

Ivan the coachman was not the only one at Kamenka to believe in the power of the local spirits. There was another Ivan, our oldest gamekeeper – Ivan Ivanovich. He had been a gamekeeper on the estate long before Sasha bought it, and he was the first to teach us the names of the most distant parts of the estate, the local legends and stories attached to streams or moors, or disused sandpits, or lonely abandoned charcoal-burners' huts. Once launched on these subjects he could go on for hours, his speech became rapid, often in whispers and he used such a selection of local expressions that it took me quite some time to understand him. He had his own names for certain districts of the forests, for thickets or mossy parts on the bogs, as well as for the weather. I often regret now that I never thought of writing them down – it was such a colourful and descriptive sort of speech.

When I first knew him, Ivan Ivanovich was already in his fifties. He was tall and thin and slightly stooping; his long measured strides were swingy as if he were always walking on the soft boggy ground of our forests. Clean shaven with greyish hair and very bushy eyebrows, clear grey eyes, weather-beaten skin and a deep low voice – this is how I still see him in my mind. He had been a sergeant in the artillery of the Guard and had retained the habit of standing to attention when talking to us. He also used military expressions when addressing us and had the soldier's manner of giving short, precise answers. His clothes were always neat, well patched, and his boots were his pride: they were made of particularly soft leather, reached far above the knees and were, according to him, entirely waterproof, having been made to order by some former military shoemaker.

At first I knew him only as the gamekeeper of the wildest district of our estate and as he lived in the village near it – some seven miles from our house – I saw him less often than the other keepers. But after the war broke out and I needed help and advice with the management of the whole place with its extensive forestry work, I learned to appreciate this man more than ever. I could trust him entirely; he was quiet and reserved and never complained of the others or tried to put himself forward. Like the other keepers he used to come twice a week to bring me the report on the work that had been done in his district, to receive money for the workmen and to get orders for the following week. If I had any spare time I could not resist the temptation of going for a day's shooting with him. It was he who had initiated me in the stalking of elk in autumn and in the approaching of capercailzie in early spring, and I felt that our long shooting rambles had made us firm friends.

Ivan Ivanovich was glad to get away from the lumber work routine, for he was a passionate hunter. His weak point was that he got so excited in the sport that he made me quite nervous too. I remember the trembling of his hand when he pointed out a capercailzie in the dark pine trees at dawn or the silhouette of an elk in the thicket in the early mornings of a misty September day. Those shooting trips of ours usually involved a night spent in the open, and it was then that he told and re-told the strangest of stories.

Ivan Ivanovich the Gamekeeper's Spirit Stories

The bright fire throws patches of light on the tall, dark fir trees, the smoke rises among their drooping branches. Not a breath of wind, crisp cold air, a light frost of a few degrees below zero.

It is past midnight, and the kettle with water boiling for our tea sings over the camp fire. Ivan Ivanovich stirs the embers with a long stick and adds a few fresh logs – sparks fly up. I lie rolled in a coat, roasting one side and still shivering in my wet clothes after the lone walk here through the bogs and the melting snow. I now dream of all those strange stories Ivan Ivanovich has been telling me. Are they true? True in the sense of being within the range of understanding of country folk, of people who live in close contact with nature? Or are they true because they have been captured by some people who feel and see and sense things which remain dead for others? Or are these stories pure imagination? Are they legends transmitted from generation to generation among these people whose life is spent among these great forests and bogs? No, they can't be only imagination, how could they be so vivid? Why should the old man who sits now in front of me invent them all? And where could he have found all the material for such colourful stories? Not in his peasant's life, not in his life as a soldier, nor – or perhaps – in his experiences as a gamekeeper?

"Yes," continues Ivan Ivanovich drowsily, poking at the fire with his stick and sending up a new firework of sparks into the black night, "no one should ever venture into those bogs beyond Veretie forests on uneven days."

"I see Friday would be wrong?" I venture hesitatingly.

"Not all Fridays; when the moon is on the decline, then one must be careful, very cautious. And then when bad omens have been sent to warn you," says Ivan Ivanovich.

"Have you ever been there, in those bogs, on uneven days?" I ask hesitatingly but driven by curiosity.

"Against my will – yes – and I had enough of it for my lifetime! It was no joke getting out of there!" he adds after a short silence.

"How did you get there against your will? By mistake, or did you lose your way?" I suggest, so as to drag the old man into a more detailed description.

"That's it. I was delayed in the forest, there had been a storm and I had to check on things after the havoc. The weather was pretty bad still – the moon on the point of disappearing. I had had bad dreams the night before – all gold coins scattered under my feet, that's no good – I knew this meant a warning, a sign to be careful. I was careful, and this saved me, thank God!" he says in a mysterious tone.

"You were in real danger then?" I ask rather reluctantly, as I feel he is not overanxious to talk about the matter.

"It's better not to talk too much about it here – this is not the right place, nor the right hour – 'they' know each other, 'they' give messages to each other from bog to bog, from forest to forest – and quickly too. The moor spirits are flighty, they may look amusing to a man who does not know them, but they are dangerous and they have a good memory. A man who escapes them once must be on the lookout whenever he comes near them – they don't forget a lost prey," and with a hard blow of his stick Ivan Ivanovich send up a fountain of sparks from the dying fire.

"Are they worse than the forest king, the Leshii?" I murmur as Ivan Ivanovich hates the name to be repeated in the open, especially at night.

"May be they are not so powerful, but they annoy and bother you to death, they drive you crazy, they are all there, surrounding you, and nowhere when you try to catch them. They wink at you with the cotton fluffy tops of the moor grasses and get you giddy with the smell of moor flowers and bushes – they are terrible!" and he shudders and looks furtively around.

The night is quiet, the fire burning cheerfully now, but I too begin to feel queer, probably from the tone of the old man's voice than from his words.

Ivan Ivanovich changes his position, readjusts his cap and puts another log on the fire.

"Do you think, Ivan Ivanovich, that they would want one's life?" I nearly whisper now, feeling that this question is really tactless.

"God alone is master over our lives, but they can hurt a man, they can lure him into their 'windows' (overgrown deep pits in bogs – remnants of former lakes) and may be it is God's will that man should perish that way."

This is conclusive, I cannot ask any more questions this time.

An owl flies noiselessly past us – Ivan Ivanovich looks up shyly, he crosses himself stealthily.

The air grows colder, dawn is approaching, the fire is dying down. Ivan Ivanovich takes out of his pocket his large silver watch.

"It's time for us to go now, my Lady, we must get to the edge of the moor from where we can hear the first song of the capercailzie, they'll start early today with this clear sky."

A few minutes later we trudge slowly through the sparse forest; I follow Ivan Ivanovich step after step, following the sound as it is still pitch dark, and I think of the uneven days and the owl warning and of all the stories the old man has been telling me in his quick half whisper, using many expressions I had never heard before.

There must be a subtler understanding of nature not given to all people; there must be more developed senses and a greater intuition in some, resembling perhaps the instinct of animals. And there must be the fine human spirit to harmonise these impressions with the deep religious feeling which still prevails among the older country people.

Coachman Ivan of Waldensee

My father's coachman in our country place in Livonia (then a province of Russia and after 1918 an independent state, Latvia) was also called Ivan, even though he was not a Russian but a Lett. I was devoted to him when I was a child, had great faith in his knowledge of horses, and spent all the time the governesses would let me have free in the stables. The best hours were in the early morning when Ivan groomed the horses and the governesses slept. Of course, as a coachman, Ivan had to know all about horses, but I felt that he was somehow afraid of them; especially afraid of riding, and this hurt my feelings very deeply, for a man should in general not be afraid of anything and as a coachman should naturally be keen on riding. Still, I respected Ivan greatly despite his weak point: he just was not a born horseman and that was not his fault, although nature had intended him to be a good rider since he had such perfect bow legs.

The other thing that puzzled me about Ivan was that my father, who was a good rider and a lover of horses, did not seem to trust Ivan entirely – neither with regard to horses (and this I instinctively understood) nor as a man – and that I only half guessed and suffered without ever daring to express my thoughts. Father was just and right and patient, and Ivan was very good too, but there was something I could not put my finger on. When I saw Ivan, standing on the terrace steps, cap in hand, crossing and re-crossing his thumbs on his stomach while taking orders from my father, I was worried. Father's strict recommendations to be back on time from the shopping trip to Wolmar, our little market town, seemed too insistent and I felt that Ivan was not quite reliable at times. Rumours had reached me of his having been drunk when out alone in town and of his bills having to be checked carefully. Still, it seemed very hard on him if he felt that lack of confidence and often, after the talk with my father, I followed Ivan to the stables and spent a few moments chatting with him just to make up for some possible ill-feeling, if there was any. Our chats were very strange when I now think back, for Ivan spoke Lettish, no Russian at all, and a very queer sort of German. So we had to use this latter language with him and I soon got into the habit of talking in infinitives as he could not understand verbs in any other form. It was great fun to practise this pigeon German on our governess, who was horrified.

Thinking back now I realise that Ivan was not quite reliable at times. Perhaps he felt that the masters could be cheated within certain limits, and not by outsiders, and he consequently kept to these limits. But I am certain that he would never have done anything greatly dishonest. His conduct in later years proved this amply.

With us children he was always patient and kind, diplomatically answering thousands of questions and becoming strict only when we crawled under the large dust covers of the carriages in the coach house, trying to get inside and to play "travelling on bad roads" with the appropriate bouncing on the driver's seat.

When in later years I came down to the old place with my own children, Ivan became in turn their devoted friend and was the first to accompany my eldest boy on his rides on the "big horses" when he left the pony to his younger brother. Only the conversations were more hampered still as my boys did not know

185

any German at that time and Ivan had not improved his Russian. But somehow they all seemed to manage very well and Ivan's patience never faltered.

The 1914 war broke out and I did not see much of Ivan for years. The Germans occupied that part of the country, then the Bolsheviks advanced. My youngest sister, who had remained in the estate as long as it was possible, was obliged to take refuge in Riga and found herself there penniless and among friends who had also fled and were hiding from socialist and communist persecution. Left to herself she took refuge in a garret and lived for months in the most distressing conditions, fetching her daily ration of soup from the popular kitchens established in the streets and sharing it with her old dog.

One day, when the revolutionary wave had passed over and the country seemed to have dammed it in for good, the coachman Ivan turned up in Riga in search of my sister. He had managed to keep my father's house from nationalisation and devastation, had settled in it himself with all his family, had gathered in his rooms all the best furniture he thought of value and had insisted with courage and energy that they were "his possessions" – a peasant's property. Socialists, communists, Germans, Russians came and went – Ivan stood his ground firmly and when order was restored he never hesitated and went in search of the last owner of the place he could trace – my youngest sister. After wandering from house to house looking up old friends and former neighbours who had fled to Riga, he discovered Mary in the garret. She was so utterly forlorn and frightened that for a long time she would not listen to him, fearing that he too was an agent of the communist bands. Finally, after much persuasion, Ivan managed to break her fear and to make her understand that he had come to fetch her and to bring her back to her own place, which still belonged to her. The difficulty was the journey as my sister had neither a winter coat nor proper shoes. Ivan decided to see to it, and three weeks later he appeared with his wife's winter coat and a pair of new high "Russian" boots which he had ordered for Mary. Again he had to coax her for quite a time before she agreed to follow him and finally he brought her home. For many years, Ivan and his wife, the good old Lisa, looked after Mary, giving her, in payment for the rent, milk, flour and eggs and tending the kitchen garden and the orchard.

Later, in the early twenties, I had to take refuge in my father's house and Ivan acted then as farmer and manager there. I spent nearly two years there with my own boys, having fled from Russia and before bringing them to Paris, and during these years Ivan never failed to offer me a lift to town when he was going there to get provisions, and in summer he willingly put his best horse at our disposal for the boys to have a drive in the country as they had had in the good old times.

It was a hard blow for him when my sisters finally had to sell the place and to emigrate abroad too. I'll never forget the day when Ivan took me to the station for the last time: tears were running down his cheeks. We both knew we would never see each other again, and he repeated in his pigeon German, "Edy, why have you all to go?", repeating my name as he used to call me in my childhood with a tone of reproach. It was one of the very painful moments in my life. When my sisters left for good, too, a couple of months later he seemed to have been quite broken-hearted. Less than a year later, he died.

The death of Ivan marked the end of our family links to Waldensee.